The Work-Smart Academic Planner

Write It Down, Get It Done

PEG DAWSON

RICHARD GUARE

THE GUILFORD PRESS
New York   London

© 2015 The Guilford Press
A Division of Guilford Publications, Inc.
370 Seventh Avenue, Suite 1200, New York, NY 10001
www.guilford.com

Printed in the United States of America

This book is printed on acid-free paper.

Last digit is print number: 9   8   7   6   5   4   3   2

ISBN 978-1-4625-1956-9

Contents

About This Planner

In our work with teenagers over many years (and through writing the *Smart but Scattered* books), we have learned that school success has less to do with how "smart" kids are than with how smart they work. Being able to manage time, plan, organize, and stay on track toward a goal (commonly called *executive skills*) has way more to do with school success than points on an IQ test.

This planner is designed not only to help you keep track of what you have to do and what deadlines you have to meet but also to help you develop the executive skills you need to achieve the kind of success you would like to experience in high school and beyond. That is why, in addition to being a place where you can keep track of daily homework assignments and due dates, this planner includes sections that help you set goals, record your successes, and create a daily study plan that fits your schedule. We also provide forms for planning how you'll tackle long-term projects and study for tests such as midterms and finals.

Since we are always looking for ways to improve what we do, we would appreciate hearing any comments or suggestions you have.

PEG DAWSON AND RICHARD GUARE
info@smartbutscatteredkids.com

Note for School Psychologists, Coaches, Educators, and Parents

- For tips on how to make the best use of this planner, please go to **www.guilford.com/work-smart-guide**.

- This planner follows the model outlined in our book *Coaching Students with Executive Skills Deficits* (The Guilford Press, 2012). For additional resources and guidance on how to coach, please refer to that book.

Using the Planner with a Coach

Before publishing this planner, we tried it out with kids to get their feedback. Here's what we learned: The teens who tried it out thought it was a *great idea*, but they had trouble using the planner consistently. Learning new skills and habits is not easy.

As you know, serious athletes work with a coach to develop their athletic skills. Even highly paid pros (such as tennis players and golfers) continue to work with coaches long after they've started earning thousands of dollars playing their sport. Coaching can help build executive skills, too.

You can use this planner by yourself, but we designed the planner to be used with an executive skills coach, who can help you get the most out of this tool.

Who can be your coach? Your school may be able to provide you with a coach. We have written a book for school professionals on coaching students around executive skills (*Coaching Students with Executive Skills Deficits*). If your school is unable to provide you with a coach, there are professional coaching resources out there, and you should discuss this with your parents. Some helpful websites are *www.adhdcoaches.org*, *www.chadd.org*, and *www.add.org*. Coaches come from a variety of professional backgrounds, including clinical or school psychology, speech pathology, occupational therapy, or the fields of special education or learning disabilities. Otherwise, a tutor, a guidance counselor, or a favorite teacher could help you learn to use this planner. You might even work with another student with strong executive skills who's being mentored by an adult.

The important thing is that you have nearly daily contact, at least at the beginning, with your coach so he or she can help you stay on track in using the planner and in following the steps outlined in the various sections.

Why bother? A lot of the things you learn in school don't stick. Let's face it, plenty of dates, names, places, and facts are forgotten as soon as the test is over. (We once saw a billboard in front of a roadside motel that said, "Another day has passed that I didn't use algebra even once.") But executive skills are actually pretty important. They're skills you need not only to be a successful student but also to be successful *for the rest of your life*. If you can develop these habits of mind while you're still in school, we promise that you will never regret a minute you spent nailing them down.

Yes, it's hard work at the start, but there *is* a huge payoff at the end. In the next section, we talk a little about executive skills and brain development, but here's an important fact about the brain: When you're learning new skills, it takes effort at first, and the brain uses up a lot of energy in the form of glucose—the fuel that powers the brain—when you practice. But the more you practice, not only do you get better at the skill, but it actually takes less effort. We know this because scientists can see that the brain uses less glucose to feed the practice. Eventually, the skills that seemed to take so much work when you started out will actually become automatic. Our hope is that by using this planner, you can make important executive skills an easy new habit.

Let's get started.

Planner Overview

This is a planner for students in grades 6–12. It is designed to help you set learning goals that work for you and to track your progress toward meeting those goals. It will also help you keep track of what you have to do and manage your time on a daily basis throughout the school year.

The planner is divided into four parts. Each part can be used independently, but working through the four sections in order will help you get the most out of the planner. A brief overview of each section follows, with more detailed instructions included at the beginning of each section.

Part I: Understanding Your Executive Skills Profile

Executive skills are brain-based skills that develop between birth and age 25 and improve with practice. They are critical to school success. They can be divided up and defined in various ways, and there are many different skills. The ones we've included in this planner are the ones that seem to matter most to success, both in school and beyond.

In this section, you will fill out a questionnaire that will help you find your strongest and weakest skills. You can then identify specific study problems associated with your weakest skills. We then offer a variety of strategies you might choose from to address your weaknesses or problem situations.

Part II: Goal Setting

Research shows that people who set goals achieve higher levels of performance than those who don't. In this section, you will have the opportunity to think about long-term goals (what you hope to do after high school), as well as shorter-term goals such as what you hope to accomplish in a single marking period. You will also be able to look back at your accomplishments at the end of the marking period and at the end of the year to assess what went well and what you might do differently the next time.

Part III: Daily/Monthly Planners

This is where you keep track of homework assignments and daily plans. It includes space for daily plans, as well as monthly planners so you don't lose sight of long-term assignments. You'll find daily planner pages for 48 weeks (the full academic year plus a few weeks in the summer) and 12 monthly planners. Use pencil to fill in the planners so that you can correct any mistakes. There are specific instructions for how to make best use of this section, including a space for a "Daily Reflection" to allow you to evaluate on a daily basis how well you are working toward your goals.

Part IV: Strategies for Success

This section includes templates, planning forms, and brief descriptions of a variety of strategies to help with things such as writing papers, planning long-term projects, studying for tests, reading for comprehension, note taking, proofreading, and staying organized.

Understanding Your Executive Skills Profile

Everyone has strengths and weaknesses in different executive skills, in the same way that everyone finds performing some kinds of tasks or learning some kinds of subject matter easier than others. Executive skills don't mature fully until at least your mid-20s, but well before that age you may recognize that you're naturally good at some things (maybe planning) but struggle with others (maybe flexibility). The more you know about your own executive skills profile, the more you can take advantage of your natural strengths while developing a game plan for improving your weaker skills.

There are three steps to understanding your own individual executive skills profile and planning how to build your executive skills based on this knowledge:

- **Step 1.** Take the **Executive Skills Questionnaire** (pages 4–5). This will enable you to identify your top two or three skills and your weakest two or three skills. You'll have a chance to refine your understanding of your executive skills weaknesses later, but take special note of your strengths, because you may be able to use them to deal with your weaknesses.

- **Step 2.** Fill out the **Executive Skills Problem Checklist** (pages 6–9). First check off every problem you think gets in the way of doing your best in school. Then go back and look at all the items you checked off and CHOOSE THREE that you think are the biggest obstacles. Review your executive skills strengths (from the **Executive Skills Questionnaire**) and think about how you might be able to use those strengths to help you academically. (For example, if you have strong goal-directed persistence, you may be able to use that to override your weakness in task initiation by telling yourself "I know what I'm working toward—getting started quickly will get me there sooner.")

- **Step 3.** When you've selected the three problems you think get in the way the most, begin thinking about how to tackle them, using the **Executive Skills Tip Sheet**. We've included definitions of each executive skill, as well as some tips for working on your weaknesses in individual tip sheets. We've included suggestions for "self-talk" because we know that what people say to themselves about a problem can have a powerful impact on how they handle that problem. It's best if you come up with your own ideas about what to tell yourself, but we've given you some suggestions.

Part I Task Completion Checklist

Task	Done (✓)
Executive Skills Questionnaire	
• Fill out the questionnaire.	_____
• Find two to three highest scores (strengths) and two to three lowest scores (weaknesses) and note them on the questionnaire.	_____
Executive Skills Problem Checklist	
• Check off all problems that affect your school performance.	_____
• Look over all identified problems and choose the three that are the biggest obstacles.	_____
• Decide on one or two that you want to select as targets and write these in the boxes at the end of the checklist.	_____
• Think about how you might be able to use your strengths to be successful and write down your ideas at the end of the checklist.	_____
Executive Skills Tip Sheets	
• Read over all the executive skills to familiarize yourself with the definitions and terms.	_____
• Locate the executive skills that correspond to the problems you identified on the Executive Skills Problem Checklist.	_____
• Highlight or circle strategies and self-talk that you think might be helpful—or add your own ideas.	_____

Coach Sign-Off (your coach signs off after you've discussed each step with him or her and completed it):

Executive Skills Questionnaire completed: _____

Problem Checklist completed: _____

Tip Sheets reviewed and strategies selected: _____

Executive Skills Questionnaire

Directions: Read each item and decide how often it's a problem for you. Then add up the three scores in each set and write that number on the **Total score** line. Use the **Key** on page 5 to determine your executive skill strengths (two to three highest scores) and weaknesses (two to three lowest scores).

Most of the time	1	Very rarely	4
Frequently	2	Never	5
Sometimes	3		

Item	Score
1. I act on impulse.	_____
2. I get in trouble for talking too much in class.	_____
3. I say things without thinking.	_____
Total score:	_____
4. I say "I'll do it later" and then forget about it.	_____
5. I forget homework assignments or forget to take home needed materials.	_____
6. I lose or misplace belongings such as coats, notebooks, sports equipment.	_____
Total score:	_____
7. I get annoyed when homework is too hard or confusing or takes too long to finish.	_____
8. I have a short fuse, am easily frustrated.	_____
9. I get upset easily when things don't go as planned.	_____
Total score:	_____
10. I have difficulty paying attention, am easily distracted.	_____
11. I run out of steam before finishing my homework.	_____
12. I have problems sticking with chores until they are done.	_____
Total score:	_____
13. I put off homework or chores until the last minute.	_____
14. It's hard for me to put aside fun activities to start homework.	_____
15. I need many reminders to start chores.	_____
Total score:	_____
16. I have trouble planning for big assignments (knowing what to do first, second, etc.).	_____
17. It's hard for me to set priorities when I have a lot of things to do.	_____
18. I become overwhelmed by long-term projects or big assignments.	_____
Total score:	_____
19. My backpack and notebooks are disorganized.	_____
20. My desk or workspace at home is a mess.	_____
21. I have trouble keeping my room tidy.	_____
Total score:	_____

Executive Skills Questionnaire (cont.)

Item	Score
22. I have a hard time estimating how long it takes to do something (such as homework).	_____
23. I often don't finish homework at night and rush to get it done in school before class.	_____
24. I'm slow getting ready for things (for example, school or appointments).	_____
Total score:	_____
25. If the first solution to a problem doesn't work, I have trouble thinking of a different one.	_____
26. It's hard for me to deal with changes in plans or routines.	_____
27. I have problems with open-ended homework assignments (for example, knowing what to write about for a creative writing assignment).	_____
Total score:	_____
28. I don't have effective study strategies.	_____
29. I don't check my work for mistakes even when the stakes are high.	_____
30. I don't evaluate my performance and change tactics to increase my success.	_____
Total score:	_____
31. I can't seem to save up money for something I want.	_____
32. I don't see the value in earning good grades to achieve a long-term goal.	_____
33. If something fun comes up when I should be studying, it's hard for me to make myself study.	_____
Total score:	_____

Key

Items	Executive Skill	Items	Executive Skill
1–3	Response inhibition	4–6	Working memory
7–9	Emotional control	10–12	Sustained attention
13–15	Task initiation	16–18	Planning/prioritization
19–21	Organization	22–24	Time management
25–27	Flexibility	28–30	Metacognition
31–33	Goal-directed persistence		

Your Executive Skill Strengths

_____

_____

_____

Your Executive Skill Weaknesses

_____

_____

_____

Executive Skills Problem Checklist

Directions:

1. **Check (✓) problem areas that significantly interfere with effective studying.**
2. **Look over all the items you checked and choose THREE that you think cause the greatest problems. Place a star (★) next to those.**

Response Inhibition

____ Rushing through work just to get it done

____ Not having the patience to produce quality work

____ Giving up on a homework assignment when I encounter an obstacle

____ Having trouble doing homework when there are more fun things to do

Working Memory

____ Writing assignment instructions without enough detail to understand later

____ Forgetting to take home necessary materials or take materials to class

____ Forgetting to hand in homework

____ Forgetting long-term projects or upcoming tests

____ Not paying attention to classroom instructions/task directions

____ Trouble remembering multiple directions or multiple problem steps

____ Losing materials

____ Forgetting to complete assignments

____ Forgetting to check agenda/assignment book

____ Not recording when an assignment is due

Emotional Control

____ Getting really irritated when a homework assignment is hard or confusing

____ Finding it hard to get started on assignments because of perfectionism or fear of failure

____ Freezing when taking tests and doing poorly despite studying long and hard

____ Not seeing the point of an assignment and finding it hard to motivate myself to do it

Task Initiation

____ Procrastinating/avoiding tasks due to:

    ____ not knowing how to get started

    ____ believing the task will "take forever"

    ____ believing my performance won't meet expectations

    ____ seeing the task as tedious, boring, or irrelevant

____ Finding other things to do rather than starting homework

____ Difficulty getting back to work after breaks

Executive Skills Problem Checklist (cont.)

Sustained Attention

____ Taking frequent breaks when working

____ Taking breaks that are too long

____ Internally distracted—thoughts, states, moods, daydreams. Please specify: _____

_____

____ Externally distracted—sights, sounds, technology such as phone, computer, TV, video games. Please specify: _____

_____

____ Rushing through work—sloppy/mistakes

____ Not knowing limits (e.g., how long I can sustain attention) or when the best study time is

____ Not recognizing when I'm off-task

Planning/Prioritization

____ Not making a study plan (or I don't know how)

____ Can't break down long-term projects into smaller tasks and timelines

____ Having difficulty taking notes or studying for tests because I can't distinguish important from unimportant

____ Not using or not knowing how to use agenda/assignment book

____ Spending too much time on less important elements—can't put the most important parts or most important assignments first

____ Planning unrealistically (for example, failing to take into account obstacles to the plan)

Flexibility

____ Struggling with assignments that require creativity or are open ended

____ Getting stuck on one solution or one way of looking at a problem

____ Having trouble coming up with topics or ideas for things to write about

____ Having difficulty coming up with "Plan B" if the first attempt didn't work

Organization

____ Not using or knowing how to design an organizational system

____ Not being able to find things in notebooks or backpacks

____ Losing assignments or important papers

____ Not having a neat study area

____ Losing electronic data—forgetting where work is stored or what name it's filed under

Executive Skills Problem Checklist (cont.)

Time Management

____ Can't estimate how long a task will take—due to:

    ____ Overestimating how long it will take to do a task (thereby never getting started)

    ____ Underestimating how long it will take to do a task (thereby running out of time)

____ Chronically late (for school, tutoring, other appointments and obligations)

____ Difficulty juggling multiple assignments and responsibilities because I can't judge time involved

____ Overcommitted—juggling too many obligations (and thinking I can pull it off)

____ Lacking a sense of time urgency (I don't appreciate that deadlines are important)

____ Relying on deadline as activator or motivator

Goal-Directed Persistence

____ Not having a long-term goal

____ Having a long-term goal but lacking a realistic plan to achieve the goal

____ Not seeing how daily actions affect goal attainment

____ Not seeing studying as important and making minimal effort as a result

____ Giving up in the face of an obstacle

____ Having a "good enough" mentality that gets in the way of producing quality work

____ "Not on the radar"—seeing work as not relevant or not important enough to do

Metacognition

____ Can't accurately evaluate skills (for example, expecting to do well on tests in spite of poor past performance; expecting to go to a college or get a job without requisite skills or academic record)

____ Can't identify appropriate study strategies

____ Can't plan or organize a writing assignment

____ Can memorize facts but miss the larger context (I do better on multiple-choice tests than essay questions)

____ Having a hard time understanding more abstract concepts (math as well as content-area subjects)

____ Having difficulty making inferences, drawing conclusions, grasping the main idea, reading between the lines

____ Failing to check work/proofread

Other

List any other things you can think of that get in the way of doing your best in school.

_____

_____

_____

_____

Executive Skills Problem Checklist (cont.)

Executive skill	Specific problem

What are some ways that I could use my executive skill strengths to help me be successful?

_____

_____

_____

_____

_____

_____

_____

_____

_____

_____

_____

Executive Skills Tip Sheets

This sheet gives definitions of each executive skill included in the Executive Skills Problem Checklist, along with tips and things you can say to yourself to get better at that skill. As you read through the suggestions, circle or highlight those ideas that you think might work for you.

Response Inhibition—being able to control your impulses so that you can think before you act, resist peer pressure, and make good choices (for example, choosing to study rather than do more appealing activities).

Tips	Self-Talk*
• Be aware of your unique temptations and make a plan to avoid them. • Ask yourself, "Good choice or bad choice?" • Practice waiting (for example, add a little more time or work before giving yourself the reward). • **Other strategies**:	• First work, then play. • Learn from your mistakes. • Stop and think. • **Your own idea:**

Working Memory—being able to keep in mind everything you have to remember—and remembering what worked the last time.

Tips	Self-Talk
• Get teachers' permission to e-mail assignments. • Do all work on iPad or tablet so it's always with you. • Use colored markers to highlight instructions (use different colors to signal different things, such as green for the most important, red for things you might be likely to forget). • Set reminders with time and sound cue on your smartphone. • Make checklists. • **Other strategies:**	• Am I forgetting anything? • Check your list. • Check your agenda. • **Your own idea:**

---

*Self-talk means giving yourself instructions, words of encouragement, or prompts to remind you what you're working on and what your goal is.

Executive Skills Tip Sheets (cont.)

Emotional Control—being able to manage your feelings so they don't get in the way of getting work done or meeting goals.

Tips	Self-Talk
• Label the feeling and let it go. • When you can, walk away from the upsetting situation, get ahold of yourself, and come back. • Look into learning meditation techniques. • Pat yourself on the back when you stay cool. • **Other strategies:**	• Take 10. • Take deep breaths. • This, too, shall pass. • Big deal or little deal? • **Your own idea:**

Sustained Attention—staying on task, getting things done in the time you've given yourself to do them, even if you're tired, bored, or have more appealing distractions.

Tips	Self-Talk
• Set realistic work goals and stick to them. • Take planned breaks and get back to work on schedule. • Gather all necessary materials before beginning a task. • Build in rewards for completing tasks. • **Other strategies:**	• You can't walk away from this. • Don't quit now. • Back to work. • First work, then play. • **Your own idea:**

Task Initiation—being able to make yourself start a task. If you've seen yourself getting closer to your goal, this is the first step on that path. If you don't take this step, you can't get closer.

Tips	Self-Talk
• Pick the task (make it small). • Pick the start time. • Pick the minimum work time. • Pick the cue to start. • **Other strategies:**	• Just do it. • Take baby steps. • Start small. • **Your own idea:**

Executive Skills Tip Sheets (cont.)

Flexibility—the ability to adapt to unexpected events and to come up with multiple solutions to problems.

Tips	Self-Talk
• Notice the physical warning signs of inflexibility (muscle tightness, breathing changes) and ask yourself if you can find a way to be flexible. • Whenever you have to make a decision about something, ask yourself, "What could go wrong and what's Plan B if this doesn't work?" • **Other strategies:**	• Big deal or little deal? • What are your options? • What's Plan B? • Is there another way to think about this? • **Your own idea:**

Planning/Prioritization—planning is your road map, your GPS. When you have a good plan, you know all the turns you have to make and how to get past the roadblocks along the way. You also know how to focus on what's most important and let the little things go.

Tips	Self-Talk
• Use the planning forms in this agenda (long-term projects; test study plan). • Ask teachers for a preview of a lecture or to tell you what are the most important concepts to focus on when studying for tests. (Teachers who provide study guides for tests make this easy!) • When you have written instructions for homework assignments, underline and number each instruction that's an *action*. • **Other strategies:**	• What's your destination? • Your plan will be a built-in GPS to get there. • Map the route. • What comes first, next, and next, and what do you need to give up to get there? • First things first. • **Your own idea:**

Organization—having a system for keeping track of information and materials, especially the things you need every day (homework, notebooks, keys, phone, sports equipment, etc.)—putting everything in its place, so when you look for it, it's there.

Tips	Self-Talk
• Use laptop or iPad for managing information/ assignments/class notes. • Use a note organizer app such as OneNote or Evernote. • Spend five minutes every day staying organized. • **Other strategies:**	• A place for everything and everything in its place. • Do you have it together? • **Your own idea:**

Executive Skills Tip Sheets *(cont.)*

Time management—Each day is a 24-hour shot clock. Time management allows you to manage the tug of war between what you want to do, what you need to do, and what others ask you to do.

Tips	Self-Talk
• Use this planner to make daily plans.	• How much time do you have?
• Estimate how long a task will take—and check to see if you were right.	• Are you on track?
• Break homework down into short time segments. (Pomodoro is a smartphone app that helps you do that.)	• What you need to do comes before what you want to do.
• **Other strategies:**	• Honestly, how long will it really take?
	• Each day is like a shot clock in a game.
	• **Your own idea:**

Goal-Directed Persistence—This is a giant version of sustained attention: You have a goal, and you're determined to get there. What you do on a day-to-day basis gets you to that goal, and keeping this in mind helps you connect immediate actions and consequences with other ones down the road.

Tips	Self-Talk
• Make daily study plans to build a sense of accomplishment.	• What are you working on?
• Set *any* goal related to schoolwork, and if the goal isn't met, make it smaller, more attainable.	• Are you on track?
	• Don't give up now.
• Place a picture of your goal in a prominent place to remind you what you're working on.	• Keep your eye on the prize.
	• Will this help you get to your goal?
• **Other strategies:**	• **Your own idea:**

Metacognition—What did I do + why did I do it = what will I do the next time? Metacognition is your brain's life lesson machine. It allows you to look at your past actions and behaviors, analyze them, and use that information to make more informed decisions about how to act in the future.

Tips	Self-Talk
• Ask teachers for a test study guide.	• What's the big picture?
• Create error-monitoring checklists (for example, a proofreading checklist).	• How are you doing?
	• What worked for you before?
• Create your own study packets for tests by pulling together all important material and stapling it together with a cover.	• What didn't?
• Ask four self-monitoring questions: "What is my problem?" "What is my plan?" "Am I following my plan?" "How did I do?"	• What do you need or want for a grade?
	• Have you studied enough to get it?
• **Other strategies:**	• **Your own idea:**

Goal Setting

We know that people who get what they want from life do so in part because they *set goals*. Goals help us because:

- They *direct behavior* (they aim us at doing what will get us where we want to go and away from distractions).

- They *energize* us.

- They encourage *persistence*.

- They *motivate* us to discover and use new knowledge and skills that get us to our goals.

Goal setting has the following steps (all found on the **Goal-Setting Worksheet**):

- Identify your long-term goal. What do you want to do after high school? Are you shooting for college or for a job? The **Goal-Setting Worksheet** gives you space to check off your choice and also to write down the college you hope to attend or the kind of job you hope to get if you know that, too.

- Next, think about what you hope to accomplish this year. You may want to list academic goals (for example, get grades of C+ or better in all my subjects, turn in 80% of my homework on time) or executive skills goals (for example, improve my time management skills, decrease procrastination). If you can do it, choose two academic and two executive skill goals to focus on.

- Now think about marking period goals. You're going to fill out this part of the worksheet at the beginning of each marking period (don't do it all at once, because the goals may change as the year goes along). First, decide on some goals tied directly to getting good grades, choosing only the one(s) you think are most important and that you're most likely to be successful at.

- Also for each marking period, think about what grades you want to earn in each subject area. Ideally, you should think about each major subject, but if that's more than you can manage, decide which classes you really want to focus on.

- At the end of the marking period, reflect on how well you did. Note what grades you were hoping to earn and what grades you actually earned. In the worksheet, jot down some ideas for what you might do differently the next marking period. You may decide you should just keep doing what you were doing.

- At the end of the year, take a few minutes to reflect on how the year went. List some things that went well and some things you want to work on next year. Keep these in mind when the next school year begins.

Part II Task Completion Checklist

Task	Done (✓)			
Decide on plans after high school (college, job, not sure).				
Decide on academic and executive skills goals for this year.				
	Q1	Q2	Q3	Q4
Decide on marking period goals (one marking period at a time).				
Set goals for report card grades (one marking period at a time).				
Look back and evaluate at the end of each marking period.				
At the end of the year, reflect on how the year went—what went well, what you might want to work on next year.				

Coach Sign-Off (your coach signs off after you've discussed each step with him or her and completed it):

Plans after high school: _____

Academic/executive skills goals set: _____

Marking period goals set:

    Q1 _____

    Q2 _____

    Q3 _____

    Q4 _____

End-of-year reflection: _____

Goal–Setting Worksheet

What are your plans for after you finish high school?

☐ College   ☐ Job   ☐ Not sure

Goals for this year: What school-related goals do you have for this year? Include academic goals and/or executive skills goals.

Academic Goal(s)	Executive Skills Goal(s)
1.	1.
2.	2.

Marking Period Goals

At the beginning of each marking period, select one or more goals to work on.

Possible Goals	1st	2nd	3rd	4th
Improve class attendance				
Improve homework completion				
Increase number of homework assignments handed in on time				
Improve grades on homework assignments				
Improve test or quiz grades				
Improve class participation				
Decrease discipline referrals				
Other: _____ _____ _____ _____				

Goal-Setting Worksheet (cont.)

At the beginning of each marking period, identify the grades you hope to earn in each subject.

Class	1st	2nd	3rd	4th

Looking Back

At the end of each marking period, compare the grades you wanted with the grades you got.

Marking Period 1

Class	Grade I wanted	Grade I got	What will I do differently next time?

19

Goal–Setting Worksheet (cont.)

Class	Grade I wanted	Grade I got	What will I do differently next time?

Marking Period 3

Class	Grade I wanted	Grade I got	What will I do differently next time?

Goal–Setting Worksheet (cont.)

Marking Period 4

Class	Grade I wanted	Grade I got	What will I do differently next time?

Goal–Setting Worksheet (cont.)

List what went well this year. Did you meet your goals? Get the grades you wanted? Learn something interesting? Improve your executive skills?

1.

2.

3.

4.

What do you want to work on next year?

1.

2.

3.

4.

PART III

Daily/Monthly Planners

This section contains two kinds of calendars:

- A daily planner where you can write down homework assignments and plan when you will do them.

- A monthly planner in which you can keep track of long-term assignments and tests and quizzes.

Daily Planner

This section is mainly for writing down homework assignments and due dates.

- To begin with, fill in the dates for each week at least a month in advance or even for the full school year (to get that task out of the way quickly). Use the reference calendar at the back of this planner or a current calendar as a guide and check your work as you go along. If you need to replace a daily planner page, you can photocopy a blank page and staple it on top.

- Decide which questions you should answer, using the following guide.

If you have problems with . . .	Answer this question in your planner
Time management	*How long* (How long do I think the assignment will take?)
Task initiation	*Start time* (When will I start the assignment?)

If you have problems with . . .	Answer this question in your planner
Working memory	*Materials* (Do I have all the materials I need to do the assignment?)
Flexibility or metacognition	*Contact* (What person should I contact if I get stuck?)

- If none of the above are problems for you, then just use the planner to write down all your assignments. If you take a picture of the homework assignment as it's written on the board, or if the details of the assignment are available online, then note that in the planner so you'll know where to find the assignment.

- Place a check mark next to the assignment as soon as you have completed it.

- Draw a line through each assignment after you have turned it in.

- Use the space at the top for general reminders, especially for things you absolutely have to remember to do that aren't directly connected to that night's homework.

- Use the Daily Reflection box at the bottom to assess, either by yourself or with your coach, how well you're meeting your daily goals. You may want to use a 1–5 scale (5—Great! Met all my goals; 4—Pretty good, 80% successful; 3—Not bad, 60% successful; 2—Some problems, 40% successful; 1—Ran into trouble, met only a small portion of my goals).

- **Check the monthly planner EVERY DAY to make sure you haven't forgotten anything due the next day.**

Monthly Planner

A blank page precedes each monthly planner. Use this to jot down anything you need to remember that month. Then you can preview the upcoming month to help you anticipate major assignments and activities that you will need to plan for.

You'll also need to fill in the dates on the monthly planner, using the reference calendars at the top of the page or the back of this planner. Any assignment that's not due *the next day* should be written on the monthly planner on the date it's due. The monthly planner comes just before the daily planner each month. No need for long explanations, just a notation so you don't forget, and perhaps include the date when it was assigned so you can go back to the spot in the daily planner for more detailed instructions. **When you're making daily homework plans, be sure to check the monthly planner to make sure you haven't forgotten anything.**

As with your daily planner, place a check mark next to each assignment written in your monthly planner as soon as you complete it and draw a line through it when you've handed it in.

Monthly Planner

August 2015

S	M	T	W	T	F	S
						1
2	3	4	5	6	7	8
9	10	11	12	13	14	15
16	17	18	19	20	21	22
23	24	25	26	27	28	29
30	31					

August 2016

S	M	T	W	T	F	S
	1	2	3	4	5	6
7	8	9	10	11	12	13
14	15	16	17	18	19	20
21	22	23	24	25	26	27
28	29	30	31			

August 2017

S	M	T	W	T	F	S
		1	2	3	4	5
6	7	8	9	10	11	12
13	14	15	16	17	18	19
20	21	22	23	24	25	26
27	28	29	30	31		

My EXECUTIVE SKILL goal:

My ACADEMIC goal:

**Be sure to check off when you've finished each assignment.
When you hand it in, cross it out!**

Sunday	Monday	Tuesday	Wednesday	Thursday	Friday	Saturday

Daily Planner

What am I working on? (Long-term goal) _____

Date: **MONDAY**	Date: **TUESDAY**	Date: **WEDNESDAY**
URGENT: REMEMBER THIS!	**URGENT: REMEMBER THIS!**	**URGENT: REMEMBER THIS!**

Subject	Due date	Subject	Due date	Subject	Due date
How long?	Start time?	How long?	Start time?	How long?	Start time?
Materials?		Materials?		Materials?	
Contact		Contact		Contact	

Subject	Due date	Subject	Due date	Subject	Due date
How long?	Start time?	How long?	Start time?	How long?	Start time?
Materials?		Materials?		Materials?	
Contact		Contact		Contact	

Subject	Due date	Subject	Due date	Subject	Due date
How long?	Start time?	How long?	Start time?	How long?	Start time?
Materials?		Materials?		Materials?	
Contact		Contact		Contact	

Subject	Due date	Subject	Due date	Subject	Due date
How long?	Start time?	How long?	Start time?	How long?	Start time?
Materials?		Materials?		Materials?	
Contact		Contact		Contact	

Daily reflection	Daily reflection	Daily reflection

Key to Questions

How long? *How long will the assignment take?*   **Start time?** *When do I plan on starting the assignment?*

Materials? *Do I have all the materials needed to complete the assignment?*   **Contact?** *Who can I contact if I get stuck?*

What am I working on? (Long-term goal)

Date: **THURSDAY**	Date: **FRIDAY**	Dates: **SATURDAY** & **SUNDAY**
URGENT: REMEMBER THIS!	**URGENT: REMEMBER THIS!**	Weekend plans/activities
Subject — Due date	Subject — Due date	
How long? — Start time? Materials?	How long? — Start time? Materials?	
Contact	Contact	
Subject — Due date	Subject — Due date	To-do list
How long? — Start time? Materials?	How long? — Start time? Materials?	
Contact	Contact	
Subject — Due date	Subject — Due date	Saturday schedule
How long? — Start time? Materials?	How long? — Start time? Materials?	
Contact	Contact	
Subject — Due date	Subject — Due date	Sunday schedule
How long? — Start time? Materials?	How long? — Start time? Materials?	
Contact	Contact	
Daily reflection	Daily reflection	Weekend reflection

Key to Questions

How long? *How long will the assignment take?*
Materials? *Do I have all the materials needed to complete the assignment?*

Start time? *When do I plan on starting the assignment?*
Contact? *Who can I contact if I get stuck?*

27

Daily Planner

What am I working on? (Long-term goal)

Date: **MONDAY**	Date: **TUESDAY**	Date: **WEDNESDAY**
URGENT: REMEMBER THIS!	**URGENT: REMEMBER THIS!**	**URGENT: REMEMBER THIS!**

MONDAY

Subject	Due date
How long?	Start time?
Materials?	
Contact	

Subject	Due date
How long?	Start time?
Materials?	
Contact	

Subject	Due date
How long?	Start time?
Materials?	
Contact	

Subject	Due date
How long?	Start time?
Materials?	
Contact	

Daily reflection

TUESDAY

Subject	Due date
How long?	Start time?
Materials?	
Contact	

Subject	Due date
How long?	Start time?
Materials?	
Contact	

Subject	Due date
How long?	Start time?
Materials?	
Contact	

Subject	Due date
How long?	Start time?
Materials?	
Contact	

Daily reflection

WEDNESDAY

Subject	Due date
How long?	Start time?
Materials?	
Contact	

Subject	Due date
How long?	Start time?
Materials?	
Contact	

Subject	Due date
How long?	Start time?
Materials?	
Contact	

Subject	Due date
How long?	Start time?
Materials?	
Contact	

Daily reflection

Key to Questions

How long? *How long will the assignment take?* **Start time?** *When do I plan on starting*
Materials? *Do I have all the materials needed*   *the assignment?*
to complete the assignment? **Contact?** *Who can I contact if I get stuck?*

What am I working on? (Long-term goal)

_____

Date: **THURSDAY**	Date: **FRIDAY**	Dates: **SATURDAY & SUNDAY**
URGENT: REMEMBER THIS!	**URGENT: REMEMBER THIS!**	Weekend plans/activities
Subject / Due date	Subject / Due date	
How long? / Start time?	How long? / Start time?	
Materials?	Materials?	
Contact	Contact	
Subject / Due date	Subject / Due date	To-do list
How long? / Start time?	How long? / Start time?	
Materials?	Materials?	
Contact	Contact	
Subject / Due date	Subject / Due date	Saturday schedule
How long? / Start time?	How long? / Start time?	
Materials?	Materials?	
Contact	Contact	
Subject / Due date	Subject / Due date	Sunday schedule
How long? / Start time?	How long? / Start time?	
Materials?	Materials?	
Contact	Contact	
Daily reflection	Daily reflection	Weekend reflection

Key to Questions

How long? _How long will the assignment take?_   **Start time?** _When do I plan on starting_
Materials? _Do I have all the materials needed_   _the assignment?_
to complete the assignment?   **Contact?** _Who can I contact if I get stuck?_

Daily Planner

Week of

What am I working on? (Long-term goal)

Date: **MONDAY**	Date: **TUESDAY**	Date: **WEDNESDAY**
URGENT: REMEMBER THIS!	**URGENT: REMEMBER THIS!**	**URGENT: REMEMBER THIS!**

Subject	Due date	Subject	Due date	Subject	Due date
How long?	Start time?	How long?	Start time?	How long?	Start time?
Materials?		Materials?		Materials?	
Contact		Contact		Contact	

Subject	Due date	Subject	Due date	Subject	Due date
How long?	Start time?	How long?	Start time?	How long?	Start time?
Materials?		Materials?		Materials?	
Contact		Contact		Contact	

Subject	Due date	Subject	Due date	Subject	Due date
How long?	Start time?	How long?	Start time?	How long?	Start time?
Materials?		Materials?		Materials?	
Contact		Contact		Contact	

Subject	Due date	Subject	Due date	Subject	Due date
How long?	Start time?	How long?	Start time?	How long?	Start time?
Materials?		Materials?		Materials?	
Contact		Contact		Contact	

Daily reflection	Daily reflection	Daily reflection

Key to Questions

How long? *How long will the assignment take?*
Materials? *Do I have all the materials needed to complete the assignment?*

Start time? *When do I plan on starting the assignment?*
Contact? *Who can I contact if I get stuck?*

What am I working on? (Long-term goal)

_____

Date: **THURSDAY**		Date: **FRIDAY**		Dates: **SATURDAY** & **SUNDAY**
URGENT: REMEMBER THIS!		**URGENT: REMEMBER THIS!**		Weekend plans/activities
Subject	Due date	Subject	Due date	
How long?	Start time?	How long?	Start time?	
Materials?		Materials?		
Contact		Contact		
Subject	Due date	Subject	Due date	To-do list
How long?	Start time?	How long?	Start time?	
Materials?		Materials?		
Contact		Contact		
Subject	Due date	Subject	Due date	Saturday schedule
How long?	Start time?	How long?	Start time?	
Materials?		Materials?		
Contact		Contact		
Subject	Due date	Subject	Due date	Sunday schedule
How long?	Start time?	How long?	Start time?	
Materials?		Materials?		
Contact		Contact		
Daily reflection		Daily reflection		Weekend reflection

Key to Questions

How long? _How long will the assignment take?_ **Start time?** _When do I plan on starting the assignment?_
Materials? _Do I have all the materials needed to complete the assignment?_ **Contact?** _Who can I contact if I get stuck?_

31

Daily Planner

Week of

What am I working on? (Long-term goal)

Date: MONDAY

URGENT: REMEMBER THIS!

Subject	Due date

How long?	Start time?

Materials?

Contact

Subject	Due date

How long?	Start time?

Materials?

Contact

Subject	Due date

How long?	Start time?

Materials?

Contact

Subject	Due date

How long?	Start time?

Materials?

Contact

Daily reflection

Date: TUESDAY

URGENT: REMEMBER THIS!

Subject	Due date

How long?	Start time?

Materials?

Contact

Subject	Due date

How long?	Start time?

Materials?

Contact

Subject	Due date

How long?	Start time?

Materials?

Contact

Subject	Due date

How long?	Start time?

Materials?

Contact

Daily reflection

Date: WEDNESDAY

URGENT: REMEMBER THIS!

Subject	Due date

How long?	Start time?

Materials?

Contact

Subject	Due date

How long?	Start time?

Materials?

Contact

Subject	Due date

How long?	Start time?

Materials?

Contact

Subject	Due date

How long?	Start time?

Materials?

Contact

Daily reflection

Key to Questions

How long? *How long will the assignment take?*
Materials? *Do I have all the materials needed to complete the assignment?*

Start time? *When do I plan on starting the assignment?*
Contact? *Who can I contact if I get stuck?*

What am I working on? (Long-term goal)

Date: **THURSDAY**		Date: **FRIDAY**		Dates: **SATURDAY** & **SUNDAY**
URGENT: REMEMBER THIS!		**URGENT: REMEMBER THIS!**		Weekend plans/activities
Subject	Due date	Subject	Due date	
How long?	Start time?	How long?	Start time?	
Materials?		Materials?		
Contact		Contact		
Subject	Due date	Subject	Due date	To-do list
How long?	Start time?	How long?	Start time?	
Materials?		Materials?		
Contact		Contact		
Subject	Due date	Subject	Due date	Saturday schedule
How long?	Start time?	How long?	Start time?	
Materials?		Materials?		
Contact		Contact		
Subject	Due date	Subject	Due date	Sunday schedule
How long?	Start time?	How long?	Start time?	
Materials?		Materials?		
Contact		Contact		
Daily reflection		Daily reflection		Weekend reflection

Key to Questions

How long? *How long will the assignment take?*
Materials? *Do I have all the materials needed to complete the assignment?*

Start time? *When do I plan on starting the assignment?*
Contact? *Who can I contact if I get stuck?*

33

Daily Planner

Week of _____

What am I working on? (Long-term goal) _____

Date: **MONDAY**	Date: **TUESDAY**	Date: **WEDNESDAY**
URGENT: REMEMBER THIS!	**URGENT: REMEMBER THIS!**	**URGENT: REMEMBER THIS!**

Subject	Due date	Subject	Due date	Subject	Due date

How long?	Start time?	How long?	Start time?	How long?	Start time?
Materials?		Materials?		Materials?	
Contact		Contact		Contact	

Subject	Due date	Subject	Due date	Subject	Due date

How long?	Start time?	How long?	Start time?	How long?	Start time?
Materials?		Materials?		Materials?	
Contact		Contact		Contact	

Subject	Due date	Subject	Due date	Subject	Due date

How long?	Start time?	How long?	Start time?	How long?	Start time?
Materials?		Materials?		Materials?	
Contact		Contact		Contact	

Subject	Due date	Subject	Due date	Subject	Due date

How long?	Start time?	How long?	Start time?	How long?	Start time?
Materials?		Materials?		Materials?	
Contact		Contact		Contact	

Daily reflection	Daily reflection	Daily reflection

Key to Questions

How long? *How long will the assignment take?*
Materials? *Do I have all the materials needed to complete the assignment?*

Start time? *When do I plan on starting the assignment?*
Contact? *Who can I contact if I get stuck?*

What am I working on? (Long-term goal)

Date: **THURSDAY**		Date: **FRIDAY**		Dates: **SATURDAY & SUNDAY**
URGENT: REMEMBER THIS!		**URGENT: REMEMBER THIS!**		Weekend plans/activities
Subject	Due date	Subject	Due date	
How long?	Start time?	How long?	Start time?	
Materials?		Materials?		
Contact		Contact		
Subject	Due date	Subject	Due date	To-do list
How long?	Start time?	How long?	Start time?	
Materials?		Materials?		
Contact		Contact		
Subject	Due date	Subject	Due date	Saturday schedule
How long?	Start time?	How long?	Start time?	
Materials?		Materials?		
Contact		Contact		
Subject	Due date	Subject	Due date	Sunday schedule
How long?	Start time?	How long?	Start time?	
Materials?		Materials?		
Contact		Contact		
Daily reflection		Daily reflection		Weekend reflection

Key to Questions

How long? *How long will the assignment take?*
Materials? *Do I have all the materials needed to complete the assignment?*

Start time? *When do I plan on starting the assignment?*
Contact? *Who can I contact if I get stuck?*

Things to Remember for Next Month

(e.g., upcoming projects; midterms, finals or major exams; start of sport season or other extracurricular activity; change in work schedule; family or class trips; school vacation)

Monthly Planner

September 2015

S	M	T	W	T	F	S
		1	2	3	4	5
6	7	8	9	10	11	12
13	14	15	16	17	18	19
20	21	22	23	24	25	26
27	28	29	30			

September 2016

S	M	T	W	T	F	S
				1	2	3
4	5	6	7	8	9	10
11	12	13	14	15	16	17
18	19	20	21	22	23	24
25	26	27	28	29	30	

September 2017

S	M	T	W	T	F	S
					1	2
3	4	5	6	7	8	9
10	11	12	13	14	15	16
17	18	19	20	21	22	23
24	25	26	27	28	29	30

My EXECUTIVE SKILL goal:

My ACADEMIC goal:

**Be sure to check off when you've finished each assignment.
When you hand it in, <u>cross it out</u>!**

Sunday	Monday	Tuesday	Wednesday	Thursday	Friday	Saturday
☐	☐	☐	☐	☐	☐	☐
☐	☐	☐	☐	☐	☐	☐
☐	☐	☐	☐	☐	☐	☐
☐	☐	☐	☐	☐	☐	☐
☐	☐	☐	☐	☐	☐	☐

Daily Planner

Week of _____ **What am I working on? (Long-term goal)** _____

Date: **MONDAY**	Date: **TUESDAY**	Date: **WEDNESDAY**
URGENT: REMEMBER THIS!	**URGENT: REMEMBER THIS!**	**URGENT: REMEMBER THIS!**

Subject / Due date	Subject / Due date	Subject / Due date
How long? / Start time?	How long? / Start time?	How long? / Start time?
Materials?	Materials?	Materials?
Contact	Contact	Contact
Subject / Due date	Subject / Due date	Subject / Due date
How long? / Start time?	How long? / Start time?	How long? / Start time?
Materials?	Materials?	Materials?
Contact	Contact	Contact
Subject / Due date	Subject / Due date	Subject / Due date
How long? / Start time?	How long? / Start time?	How long? / Start time?
Materials?	Materials?	Materials?
Contact	Contact	Contact
Subject / Due date	Subject / Due date	Subject / Due date
How long? / Start time?	How long? / Start time?	How long? / Start time?
Materials?	Materials?	Materials?
Contact	Contact	Contact
Daily reflection	Daily reflection	Daily reflection

Key to Questions

How long? *How long will the assignment take?*
Materials? *Do I have all the materials needed to complete the assignment?*

Start time? *When do I plan on starting the assignment?*
Contact? *Who can I contact if I get stuck?*

What am I working on? (Long-term goal)

_____

Date: **THURSDAY**		Date: **FRIDAY**		Dates: **SATURDAY** & **SUNDAY**
URGENT: REMEMBER THIS!		**URGENT: REMEMBER THIS!**		Weekend plans/activities
Subject	Due date	Subject	Due date	
How long?	Start time?	How long?	Start time?	
Materials?		Materials?		
Contact		Contact		
Subject	Due date	Subject	Due date	To-do list
How long?	Start time?	How long?	Start time?	
Materials?		Materials?		
Contact		Contact		
Subject	Due date	Subject	Due date	Saturday schedule
How long?	Start time?	How long?	Start time?	
Materials?		Materials?		
Contact		Contact		
Subject	Due date	Subject	Due date	Sunday schedule
How long?	Start time?	How long?	Start time?	
Materials?		Materials?		
Contact		Contact		
Daily reflection		Daily reflection		Weekend reflection

Key to Questions

How long? _How long will the assignment take?_
Materials? _Do I have all the materials needed to complete the assignment?_

Start time? _When do I plan on starting the assignment?_
Contact? _Who can I contact if I get stuck?_

Daily Planner

Week of

What am I working on? (Long-term goal)

Date: **MONDAY**	Date: **TUESDAY**	Date: **WEDNESDAY**
URGENT: REMEMBER THIS!	**URGENT: REMEMBER THIS!**	**URGENT: REMEMBER THIS!**

Subject	Due date	Subject	Due date	Subject	Due date

How long?	Start time?	How long?	Start time?	How long?	Start time?
Materials?		Materials?		Materials?	
Contact		Contact		Contact	

Subject	Due date	Subject	Due date	Subject	Due date

How long?	Start time?	How long?	Start time?	How long?	Start time?
Materials?		Materials?		Materials?	
Contact		Contact		Contact	

Subject	Due date	Subject	Due date	Subject	Due date

How long?	Start time?	How long?	Start time?	How long?	Start time?
Materials?		Materials?		Materials?	
Contact		Contact		Contact	

Subject	Due date	Subject	Due date	Subject	Due date

How long?	Start time?	How long?	Start time?	How long?	Start time?
Materials?		Materials?		Materials?	
Contact		Contact		Contact	

Daily reflection	Daily reflection	Daily reflection

Key to Questions

How long? *How long will the assignment take?*
Materials? *Do I have all the materials needed to complete the assignment?*

Start time? *When do I plan on starting the assignment?*
Contact? *Who can I contact if I get stuck?*

What am I working on? (Long-term goal)

Date: **THURSDAY**		Date: **FRIDAY**		Dates: **SATURDAY** & **SUNDAY**
URGENT: REMEMBER THIS!		**URGENT: REMEMBER THIS!**		Weekend plans/activities
Subject	Due date	Subject	Due date	
How long?	Start time?	How long?	Start time?	
Materials?		Materials?		
Contact		Contact		
Subject	Due date	Subject	Due date	To-do list
How long?	Start time?	How long?	Start time?	
Materials?		Materials?		
Contact		Contact		
Subject	Due date	Subject	Due date	Saturday schedule
How long?	Start time?	How long?	Start time?	
Materials?		Materials?		
Contact		Contact		
Subject	Due date	Subject	Due date	Sunday schedule
How long?	Start time?	How long?	Start time?	
Materials?		Materials?		
Contact		Contact		
Daily reflection		Daily reflection		Weekend reflection

Key to Questions

How long? *How long will the assignment take?*
Materials? *Do I have all the materials needed to complete the assignment?*

Start time? *When do I plan on starting the assignment?*
Contact? *Who can I contact if I get stuck?*

Daily Planner

Week of
_____

What am I working on? (Long-term goal)
_____

Date: **MONDAY**	Date: **TUESDAY**	Date: **WEDNESDAY**
URGENT: REMEMBER THIS!	**URGENT: REMEMBER THIS!**	**URGENT: REMEMBER THIS!**

Subject	Due date	Subject	Due date	Subject	Due date
How long?	Start time?	How long?	Start time?	How long?	Start time?
Materials?		Materials?		Materials?	
Contact		Contact		Contact	

Subject	Due date	Subject	Due date	Subject	Due date
How long?	Start time?	How long?	Start time?	How long?	Start time?
Materials?		Materials?		Materials?	
Contact		Contact		Contact	

Subject	Due date	Subject	Due date	Subject	Due date
How long?	Start time?	How long?	Start time?	How long?	Start time?
Materials?		Materials?		Materials?	
Contact		Contact		Contact	

Subject	Due date	Subject	Due date	Subject	Due date
How long?	Start time?	How long?	Start time?	How long?	Start time?
Materials?		Materials?		Materials?	
Contact		Contact		Contact	

Daily reflection	Daily reflection	Daily reflection

Key to Questions

How long? *How long will the assignment take?*
Materials? *Do I have all the materials needed to complete the assignment?*
Start time? *When do I plan on starting the assignment?*
Contact? *Who can I contact if I get stuck?*

What am I working on? (Long-term goal)

_____

Date: **THURSDAY**	Date: **FRIDAY**	Dates: **SATURDAY** & **SUNDAY**
URGENT: REMEMBER THIS!	**URGENT: REMEMBER THIS!**	Weekend plans/activities
Subject — Due date	Subject — Due date	
How long? — Start time? Materials? Contact	How long? — Start time? Materials? Contact	
Subject — Due date	Subject — Due date	To-do list
How long? — Start time? Materials? Contact	How long? — Start time? Materials? Contact	
Subject — Due date	Subject — Due date	Saturday schedule
How long? — Start time? Materials? Contact	How long? — Start time? Materials? Contact	
Subject — Due date	Subject — Due date	Sunday schedule
How long? — Start time? Materials? Contact	How long? — Start time? Materials? Contact	
Daily reflection	Daily reflection	Weekend reflection

Key to Questions

How long? _How long will the assignment take?_
Materials? _Do I have all the materials needed to complete the assignment?_

Start time? _When do I plan on starting the assignment?_
Contact? _Who can I contact if I get stuck?_

43

Daily Planner

Week of	What am I working on? (Long-term goal)

Date: **MONDAY**	Date: **TUESDAY**	Date: **WEDNESDAY**
URGENT: REMEMBER THIS!	**URGENT: REMEMBER THIS!**	**URGENT: REMEMBER THIS!**

Subject	Due date	Subject	Due date	Subject	Due date
How long?	Start time?	How long?	Start time?	How long?	Start time?
Materials?		Materials?		Materials?	
Contact		Contact		Contact	

Subject	Due date	Subject	Due date	Subject	Due date
How long?	Start time?	How long?	Start time?	How long?	Start time?
Materials?		Materials?		Materials?	
Contact		Contact		Contact	

Subject	Due date	Subject	Due date	Subject	Due date
How long?	Start time?	How long?	Start time?	How long?	Start tlme?
Materials?		Materials?		Materials?	
Contact		Contact		Contact	

Subject	Due date	Subject	Due date	Subject	Due date
How long?	Start time?	How long?	Start time?	How long?	Start time?
Materials?		Materials?		Materials?	
Contact		Contact		Contact	

Daily reflection	Daily reflection	Daily reflection

Key to Questions

How long? *How long will the assignment take?*   **Start time?** *When do I plan on starting the assignment?*

Materials? *Do I have all the materials needed to complete the assignment?*   **Contact?** *Who can I contact if I get stuck?*

What am I working on? (Long-term goal)

Date: **THURSDAY**		Date: **FRIDAY**		Dates: **SATURDAY** & **SUNDAY**
URGENT: REMEMBER THIS!		**URGENT: REMEMBER THIS!**		Weekend plans/activities
Subject	Due date	Subject	Due date	
How long?	Start time?	How long?	Start time?	
Materials?		Materials?		
Contact		Contact		
Subject	Due date	Subject	Due date	To-do list
How long?	Start time?	How long?	Start time?	
Materials?		Materials?		
Contact		Contact		
Subject	Due date	Subject	Due date	Saturday schedule
How long?	Start time?	How long?	Start time?	
Materials?		Materials?		
Contact		Contact		
Subject	Due date	Subject	Due date	Sunday schedule
How long?	Start time?	How long?	Start time?	
Materials?		Materials?		
Contact		Contact		
Daily reflection		Daily reflection		Weekend reflection

Key to Questions

How long? *How long will the assignment take?*
Materials? *Do I have all the materials needed to complete the assignment?*

Start time? *When do I plan on starting the assignment?*
Contact? *Who can I contact if I get stuck?*

(e.g., upcoming projects; midterms, finals or major exams; start of sport season or other extracurricular activity; change in work schedule; family or class trips; school vacation)

Monthly Planner

October 2015

S	M	T	W	T	F	S
				1	2	3
4	5	6	7	8	9	10
11	12	13	14	15	16	17
18	19	20	21	22	23	24
25	26	27	28	29	30	31

October 2016

S	M	T	W	T	F	S
						1
2	3	4	5	6	7	8
9	10	11	12	13	14	15
16	17	18	19	20	21	22
23	24	25	26	27	28	29
30	31					

October 2017

S	M	T	W	T	F	S
1	2	3	4	5	6	7
8	9	10	11	12	13	14
15	16	17	18	19	20	21
22	23	24	25	26	27	28
29	30	31				

My EXECUTIVE SKILL goal:

My ACADEMIC goal:

**Be sure to check off when you've finished each assignment.
When you hand it in, cross it out!**

Sunday	Monday	Tuesday	Wednesday	Thursday	Friday	Saturday

Daily Planner

<table>
<tr><td>Week of</td><td colspan="2">What am I working on? (Long-term goal)</td></tr>
</table>

Date: **MONDAY**	Date: **TUESDAY**	Date: **WEDNESDAY**
URGENT: REMEMBER THIS!	**URGENT: REMEMBER THIS!**	**URGENT: REMEMBER THIS!**
Subject Due date	Subject Due date	Subject Due date
How long? Start time?	How long? Start time?	How long? Start time?
Materials?	Materials?	Materials?
Contact	Contact	Contact
Subject Due date	Subject Due date	Subject Due date
How long? Start time?	How long? Start time?	How long? Start time?
Materials?	Materials?	Materials?
Contact	Contact	Contact
Subject Due date	Subject Due date	Subject Due date
How long? Start time?	How long? Start time?	How long? Start time?
Materials?	Materials?	Materials?
Contact	Contact	Contact
Subject Due date	Subject Due date	Subject Due date
How long? Start time?	How long? Start time?	How long? Start time?
Materials?	Materials?	Materials?
Contact	Contact	Contact
Daily reflection	Daily reflection	Daily reflection

Key to Questions

How long? *How long will the assignment take?*

Materials? *Do I have all the materials needed to complete the assignment?*

Start time? *When do I plan on starting the assignment?*

Contact? *Who can I contact if I get stuck?*

What am I working on? (Long-term goal)

Date: **THURSDAY**		Date: **FRIDAY**		Dates: **SATURDAY** & **SUNDAY**
URGENT: REMEMBER THIS!		**URGENT: REMEMBER THIS!**		Weekend plans/activities
Subject	Due date	Subject	Due date	
How long?	Start time?	How long?	Start time?	
Materials?		Materials?		
Contact		Contact		
Subject	Due date	Subject	Due date	To-do list
How long?	Start time?	How long?	Start time?	
Materials?		Materials?		
Contact		Contact		
Subject	Due date	Subject	Due date	Saturday schedule
How long?	Start time?	How long?	Start time?	
Materials?		Materials?		
Contact		Contact		
Subject	Due date	Subject	Due date	Sunday schedule
How long?	Start timo?	How long?	Start time?	
Materials?		Materials?		
Contact		Contact		
Daily reflection		Daily reflection		Weekend reflection

Key to Questions

How long? *How long will the assignment take?*
Materials? *Do I have all the materials needed to complete the assignment?*

Start time? *When do I plan on starting the assignment?*
Contact? *Who can I contact if I get stuck?*

Daily Planner

Week of	What am I working on? (Long-term goal)

Date: **MONDAY**	Date: **TUESDAY**	Date: **WEDNESDAY**
URGENT: REMEMBER THIS!	**URGENT: REMEMBER THIS!**	**URGENT: REMEMBER THIS!**
Subject / Due date	Subject / Due date	Subject / Due date
How long? / Start time?	How long? / Start time?	How long? / Start time?
Materials?	Materials?	Materials?
Contact	Contact	Contact
Subject / Due date	Subject / Due date	Subject / Due date
How long? / Start time?	How long? / Start time?	How long? / Start time?
Materials?	Materials?	Materials?
Contact	Contact	Contact
Subject / Due date	Subject / Due date	Subject / Due date
How long? / Start time?	How long? / Start time?	How long? / Start time?
Materials?	Materials?	Materials?
Contact	Contact	Contact
Subject / Due date	Subject / Due date	Subject / Due date
How long? / Start time?	How long? / Start time?	How long? / Start time?
Materials?	Materials?	Materials?
Contact	Contact	Contact
Daily reflection	Daily reflection	Daily reflection

Key to Questions

How long? *How long will the assignment take?*   **Start time?** *When do I plan on starting*
Materials? *Do I have all the materials needed*   *the assignment?*
to complete the assignment?   **Contact?** *Who can I contact if I get stuck?*

What am I working on? (Long-term goal)

_____

Date: **THURSDAY**	Date: **FRIDAY**	Dates: **SATURDAY & SUNDAY**
URGENT: REMEMBER THIS!	**URGENT: REMEMBER THIS!**	Weekend plans/activities
Subject / Due date	Subject / Due date	
How long? / Start time?	How long? / Start time?	
Materials?	Materials?	
Contact	Contact	
Subject / Due date	Subject / Due date	To-do list
How long? / Start time?	How long? / Start time?	
Materials?	Materials?	
Contact	Contact	
Subject / Due date	Subject / Due date	Saturday schedule
How long? / Start time?	How long? / Start time?	
Materials?	Materials?	
Contact	Contact	
Subject / Due date	Subject / Due date	Sunday schedule
How long? / Start time?	How long? / Start time?	
Materials?	Materials?	
Contact	Contact	
Daily reflection	Daily reflection	Weekend reflection

Key to Questions

How long? *How long will the assignment take?*
Materials? *Do I have all the materials needed to complete the assignment?*

Start time? *When do I plan on starting the assignment?*
Contact? *Who can I contact if I get stuck?*

Daily Planner

Week of	What am I working on? (Long-term goal)

Date: **MONDAY**	Date: **TUESDAY**	Date: **WEDNESDAY**
URGENT: REMEMBER THIS!	**URGENT: REMEMBER THIS!**	**URGENT: REMEMBER THIS!**

Subject	Due date	Subject	Due date	Subject	Due date
How long?	Start time?	How long?	Start time?	How long?	Start time?
Materials?		Materials?		Materials?	
Contact		Contact		Contact	

Subject	Due date	Subject	Due date	Subject	Due date
How long?	Start time?	How long?	Start time?	How long?	Start time?
Materials?		Materials?		Materials?	
Contact		Contact		Contact	

Subject	Due date	Subject	Due date	Subject	Due date
How long?	Start time?	How long?	Start time?	How long?	Start time?
Materials?		Materials?		Materials?	
Contact		Contact		Contact	

Subject	Due date	Subject	Due date	Subject	Due date
How long?	Start time?	How long?	Start time?	How long?	Start time?
Materials?		Materials?		Materials?	
Contact		Contact		Contact	

Daily reflection	Daily reflection	Daily reflection

Key to Questions

How long? *How long will the assignment take?*

Materials? *Do I have all the materials needed to complete the assignment?*

Start time? *When do I plan on starting the assignment?*

Contact? *Who can I contact if I get stuck?*

52

What am I working on? (Long-term goal)

Date: **THURSDAY**	Date: **FRIDAY**	Dates: **SATURDAY** & **SUNDAY**
URGENT: REMEMBER THIS!	**URGENT: REMEMBER THIS!**	Weekend plans/activities
Subject / Due date	Subject / Due date	
How long? / Start time?	How long? / Start time?	
Materials?	Materials?	
Contact	Contact	
Subject / Due date	Subject / Due date	To-do list
How long? / Start time?	How long? / Start time?	
Materials?	Materials?	
Contact	Contact	
Subject / Due date	Subject / Due date	Saturday schedule
How long? / Start time?	How long? / Start time?	
Materials?	Materials?	
Contact	Contact	
Subject / Due date	Subject / Due date	Sunday schedule
How long? / Start time?	How long? / Start time?	
Materials?	Materials?	
Contact	Contact	
Daily reflection	Daily reflection	Weekend reflection

Key to Questions

How long? *How long will the assignment take?*
Materials? *Do I have all the materials needed to complete the assignment?*

Start time? *When do I plan on starting the assignment?*
Contact? *Who can I contact if I get stuck?*

Daily Planner

Week of

What am I working on? (Long-term goal)

Date: **MONDAY**	Date: **TUESDAY**	Date: **WEDNESDAY**
URGENT: REMEMBER THIS!	**URGENT: REMEMBER THIS!**	**URGENT: REMEMBER THIS!**

Subject	Due date	Subject	Due date	Subject	Due date
How long?	Start time?	How long?	Start time?	How long?	Start time?
Materials?		Materials?		Materials?	
Contact		Contact		Contact	
Subject	Due date	Subject	Due date	Subject	Due date
How long?	Start time?	How long?	Start time?	How long?	Start time?
Materials?		Materials?		Materials?	
Contact		Contact		Contact	
Subject	Due date	Subject	Due date	Subject	Due date
How long?	Start time?	How long?	Start time?	How long?	Start time?
Materials?		Materials?		Materials?	
Contact		Contact		Contact	
Subject	Due date	Subject	Due date	Subject	Due date
How long?	Start time?	How long?	Start time?	How long?	Start time?
Materials?		Materials?		Materials?	
Contact		Contact		Contact	
Daily reflection		Daily reflection		Daily reflection	

Key to Questions

How long? *How long will the assignment take?*
Materials? *Do I have all the materials needed to complete the assignment?*
Start time? *When do I plan on starting the assignment?*
Contact? *Who can I contact if I get stuck?*

What am I working on? (Long-term goal)

Date: **THURSDAY**	Date: **FRIDAY**	Dates: **SATURDAY** & **SUNDAY**
URGENT: REMEMBER THIS!	**URGENT: REMEMBER THIS!**	Weekend plans/activities
Subject / Due date	Subject / Due date	
How long? / Start time? Materials? Contact	How long? / Start time? Materials? Contact	
Subject / Due date	Subject / Due date	To-do list
How long? / Start time? Materials? Contact	How long? / Start time? Materials? Contact	
Subject / Due date	Subject / Due date	Saturday schedule
How long? / Start time? Materials? Contact	How long? / Start time? Materials? Contact	
Subject / Due date	Subject / Due date	Sunday schedule
How long? / Start time? Materials? Contact	How long? / Start time? Materials? Contact	
Daily reflection	Daily reflection	Weekend reflection

Key to Questions

How long? *How long will the assignment take?*
Materials? *Do I have all the materials needed to complete the assignment?*

Start time? *When do I plan on starting the assignment?*
Contact? *Who can I contact if I get stuck?*

Daily Planner

Week of
_____

What am I working on? (Long-term goal)
_____

Date: **MONDAY**	Date: **TUESDAY**	Date: **WEDNESDAY**
URGENT: REMEMBER THIS!	**URGENT: REMEMBER THIS!**	**URGENT: REMEMBER THIS!**

Subject	Due date	Subject	Due date	Subject	Due date
How long?	Start time?	How long?	Start time?	How long?	Start time?
Materials?		Materials?		Materials?	
Contact		Contact		Contact	
Subject	Due date	Subject	Due date	Subject	Due date
How long?	Start time?	How long?	Start time?	How long?	Start time?
Materials?		Materials?		Materials?	
Contact		Contact		Contact	
Subject	Due date	Subject	Due date	Subject	Due date
How long?	Start time?	How long?	Start time?	How long?	Start time?
Materials?		Materials?		Materials?	
Contact		Contact		Contact	
Subject	Due date	Subject	Due date	Subject	Due date
How long?	Start time?	How long?	Start time?	How long?	Start time?
Materials?		Materials?		Materials?	
Contact		Contact		Contact	
Daily reflection		Daily reflection		Daily reflection	

Key to Questions

How long? _How long will the assignment take?_
Materials? _Do I have all the materials needed to complete the assignment?_
Start time? _When do I plan on starting the assignment?_
Contact? _Who can I contact if I get stuck?_

What am I working on? (Long-term goal)

Date: **THURSDAY**		Date: **FRIDAY**		Dates: **SATURDAY** & **SUNDAY**
URGENT: REMEMBER THIS!		**URGENT: REMEMBER THIS!**		Weekend plans/activities
Subject	Due date	Subject	Due date	
How long?	Start time?	How long?	Start time?	
Materials?		Materials?		
Contact		Contact		
Subject	Due date	Subject	Due date	To-do list
How long?	Start time?	How long?	Start time?	
Materials?		Materials?		
Contact		Contact		
Subject	Due date	Subject	Due date	Saturday schedule
How long?	Start time?	How long?	Start time?	
Materials?		Materials?		
Contact		Contact		
Subject	Due date	Subject	Due date	Sunday schedule
How long?	Start time?	How long?	Start time?	
Materials?		Materials?		
Contact		Contact		
Daily reflection		Daily reflection		Weekend reflection

Key to Questions

How long? *How long will the assignment take?*
Materials? *Do I have all the materials needed to complete the assignment?*

Start time? *When do I plan on starting the assignment?*
Contact? *Who can I contact if I get stuck?*

Things to Remember for Next Month

(e.g., upcoming projects; midterms, finals or major exams; start of sport season or other extracurricular activity; change in work schedule; family or class trips; school vacation)

Monthly Planner

November 2015

S	M	T	W	T	F	S
1	2	3	4	5	6	7
8	9	10	11	12	13	14
15	16	17	18	19	20	21
22	23	24	25	26	27	28
29	30					

November 2016

S	M	T	W	T	F	S
		1	2	3	4	5
6	7	8	9	10	11	12
13	14	15	16	17	18	19
20	21	22	23	24	25	26
27	28	29	30			

November 2017

S	M	T	W	T	F	S
			1	2	3	4
5	6	7	8	9	10	11
12	13	14	15	16	17	18
19	20	21	22	23	24	25
26	27	28	29	30		

My EXECUTIVE SKILL goal:

My ACADEMIC goal:

**Be sure to check off when you've finished each assignment.
When you hand it in, cross it out!**

Sunday	Monday	Tuesday	Wednesday	Thursday	Friday	Saturday

Daily Planner

Week of	What am I working on? (Long-term goal)

Date: **MONDAY**	Date: **TUESDAY**	Date: **WEDNESDAY**
URGENT: REMEMBER THIS!	**URGENT: REMEMBER THIS!**	**URGENT: REMEMBER THIS!**

Subject	Due date	Subject	Due date	Subject	Due date
How long?	Start time?	How long?	Start time?	How long?	Start time?
Materials?		Materials?		Materials?	
Contact		Contact		Contact	

Subject	Due date	Subject	Due date	Subject	Due date
How long?	Start time?	How long?	Start time?	How long?	Start time?
Materials?		Materials?		Materials?	
Contact		Contact		Contact	

Subject	Due date	Subject	Due date	Subject	Due date
How long?	Start time?	How long?	Start time?	How long?	Start time?
Materials?		Materials?		Materials?	
Contact		Contact		Contact	

Subject	Due date	Subject	Due date	Subject	Due date
How long?	Start time?	How long?	Start time?	How long?	Start time?
Materials?		Materials?		Materials?	
Contact		Contact		Contact	

Daily reflection	Daily reflection	Daily reflection

Key to Questions

How long? *How long will the assignment take?* **Start time?** *When do I plan on starting*
Materials? *Do I have all the materials needed* *the assignment?*
to complete the assignment? **Contact?** *Who can I contact if I get stuck?*

What am I working on? (Long-term goal)

Date: **THURSDAY**	Date: **FRIDAY**	Dates: **SATURDAY** & **SUNDAY**
URGENT: REMEMBER THIS!	**URGENT: REMEMBER THIS!**	Weekend plans/activities
Subject / Due date	Subject / Due date	
How long? / Start time?	How long? / Start time?	
Materials?	Materials?	
Contact	Contact	
Subject / Due date	Subject / Due date	To-do list
How long? / Start time?	How long? / Start time?	
Materials?	Materials?	
Contact	Contact	
Subject / Due date	Subject / Due date	Saturday schedule
How long? / Start time?	How long? / Start time?	
Materials?	Materials?	
Contact	Contact	
Subject / Due date	Subject / Due date	Sunday schedule
How long? / Start time?	How long? / Start time?	
Materials?	Materials?	
Contact	Contact	
Daily reflection	Daily reflection	Weekend reflection

Key to Questions

How long? *How long will the assignment take?*
Materials? *Do I have all the materials needed to complete the assignment?*

Start time? *When do I plan on starting the assignment?*
Contact? *Who can I contact if I get stuck?*

Daily Planner

Week of
_____

What am I working on? (Long-term goal)
_____

Date: **MONDAY**	Date: **TUESDAY**	Date: **WEDNESDAY**
URGENT: REMEMBER THIS!	**URGENT: REMEMBER THIS!**	**URGENT: REMEMBER THIS!**

MONDAY		TUESDAY		WEDNESDAY	
Subject	Due date	Subject	Due date	Subject	Due date
How long?	Start time?	How long?	Start time?	How long?	Start time?
Materials?		Materials?		Materials?	
Contact		Contact		Contact	
Subject	Due date	Subject	Due date	Subject	Due date
How long?	Start time?	How long?	Start time?	How long?	Start time?
Materials?		Materials?		Materials?	
Contact		Contact		Contact	
Subject	Due date	Subject	Due date	Subject	Due date
How long?	Start time?	How long?	Start time?	How long?	Start time?
Materials?		Materials?		Materials?	
Contact		Contact		Contact	
Subject	Due date	Subject	Due date	Subject	Due date
How long?	Start time?	How long?	Start time?	How long?	Start time?
Materials?		Materials?		Materials?	
Contact		Contact		Contact	
Daily reflection		Daily reflection		Daily reflection	

Key to Questions

How long? _How long will the assignment take?_

Materials? _Do I have all the materials needed to complete the assignment?_

Start time? _When do I plan on starting the assignment?_

Contact? _Who can I contact if I get stuck?_

What am I working on? (Long-term goal)

Date: **THURSDAY**		Date: **FRIDAY**		Dates: **SATURDAY** & **SUNDAY**
URGENT: REMEMBER THIS!		**URGENT: REMEMBER THIS!**		Weekend plans/activities
Subject	Due date	Subject	Due date	
How long?	Start time?	How long?	Start time?	
Materials?		Materials?		
Contact		Contact		
Subject	Due date	Subject	Due date	To-do list
How long?	Start time?	How long?	Start time?	
Materials?		Materials?		
Contact		Contact		
Subject	Due date	Subject	Due date	Saturday schedule
How long?	Start time?	How long?	Start time?	
Materials?		Materials?		
Contact		Contact		
Subject	Due date	Subject	Due date	Sunday schedule
How long?	Start time?	How long?	Start time?	
Materials?		Materials?		
Contact		Contact		
Daily reflection		Daily reflection		Weekend reflection

Key to Questions

How long? *How long will the assignment take?*
Materials? *Do I have all the materials needed to complete the assignment?*

Start time? *When do I plan on starting the assignment?*
Contact? *Who can I contact if I get stuck?*

Daily Planner

Week of	What am I working on? (Long-term goal)

Date: **MONDAY**	Date: **TUESDAY**	Date: **WEDNESDAY**
URGENT: REMEMBER THIS!	**URGENT: REMEMBER THIS!**	**URGENT: REMEMBER THIS!**

Subject	Due date	Subject	Due date	Subject	Due date
How long?	Start time?	How long?	Start time?	How long?	Start time?
Materials?		Materials?		Materials?	
Contact		Contact		Contact	
Subject	Due date	Subject	Due date	Subject	Due date
How long?	Start time?	How long?	Start time?	How long?	Start time?
Materials?		Materials?		Materials?	
Contact		Contact		Contact	
Subject	Due date	Subject	Due date	Subject	Due date
How long?	Start time?	How long?	Start time?	How long?	Start time?
Materials?		Materials?		Materials?	
Contact		Contact		Contact	
Subject	Due date	Subject	Due date	Subject	Due date
How long?	Start time?	How long?	Start time?	How long?	Start time?
Materials?		Materials?		Materials?	
Contact		Contact		Contact	
Daily reflection		Daily reflection		Daily reflection	

Key to Questions

How long? *How long will the assignment take?*
Materials? *Do I have all the materials needed to complete the assignment?*

Start time? *When do I plan on starting the assignment?*
Contact? *Who can I contact if I get stuck?*

What am I working on? (Long-term goal)

Date: **THURSDAY**	Date: **FRIDAY**	Dates: **SATURDAY & SUNDAY**
URGENT: REMEMBER THIS!	**URGENT: REMEMBER THIS!**	Weekend plans/activities
Subject / Due date	Subject / Due date	
How long? / Start time?	How long? / Start time?	
Materials?	Materials?	
Contact	Contact	
Subject / Due date	Subject / Due date	To-do list
How long? / Start time?	How long? / Start time?	
Materials?	Materials?	
Contact	Contact	
Subject / Due date	Subject / Due date	Saturday schedule
How long? / Start time?	How long? / Start time?	
Materials?	Materials?	
Contact	Contact	
Subject / Due date	Subject / Due date	Sunday schedule
How long? / Start time?	How long? / Start time?	
Materials?	Materials?	
Contact	Contact	
Daily reflection	Daily reflection	Weekend reflection

Key to Questions

How long? *How long will the assignment take?*   **Start time?** *When do I plan on starting*
Materials? *Do I have all the materials needed*   *the assignment?*
     to complete the assignment?   **Contact?** *Who can I contact if I get stuck?*

Daily Planner

Week of	What am I working on? (Long-term goal)
_____	_____

Date: **MONDAY**	Date: **TUESDAY**	Date: **WEDNESDAY**
URGENT: REMEMBER THIS!	**URGENT: REMEMBER THIS!**	**URGENT: REMEMBER THIS!**

Subject	Due date	Subject	Due date	Subject	Due date
How long?	Start time?	How long?	Start time?	How long?	Start time?
Materials?		Materials?		Materials?	
Contact		Contact		Contact	

Subject	Due date	Subject	Due date	Subject	Due date
How long?	Start time?	How long?	Start time?	How long?	Start time?
Materials?		Materials?		Materials?	
Contact		Contact		Contact	

Subject	Due date	Subject	Due date	Subject	Due date
How long?	Start time?	How long?	Start time?	How long?	Start time?
Materials?		Materials?		Materials?	
Contact		Contact		Contact	

Subject	Due date	Subject	Due date	Subject	Due date
How long?	Start time?	How long?	Start time?	How long?	Start time?
Materials?		Materials?		Materials?	
Contact		Contact		Contact	

Daily reflection	Daily reflection	Daily reflection

Key to Questions

How long? *How long will the assignment take?*
Materials? *Do I have all the materials needed to complete the assignment?*

Start time? *When do I plan on starting the assignment?*
Contact? *Who can I contact if I get stuck?*

What am I working on? (Long-term goal)

Date: **THURSDAY**		Date: **FRIDAY**		Dates: **SATURDAY** & **SUNDAY**
URGENT: REMEMBER THIS!		**URGENT: REMEMBER THIS!**		Weekend plans/activities
Subject	Due date	Subject	Due date	
How long?	Start time?	How long?	Start time?	
Materials?		Materials?		
Contact		Contact		
Subject	Due date	Subject	Due date	To-do list
How long?	Start time?	How long?	Start time?	
Materials?		Materials?		
Contact		Contact		
Subject	Due date	Subject	Due date	Saturday schedule
How long?	Start time?	How long?	Start time?	
Materials?		Materials?		
Contact		Contact		
Subject	Due date	Subject	Due date	Sunday schedule
How long?	Start time?	How long?	Start time?	
Materials?		Materials?		
Contact		Contact		
Daily reflection		Daily reflection		Weekend reflection

Key to Questions

How long? *How long will the assignment take?*
Materials? *Do I have all the materials needed to complete the assignment?*

Start time? *When do I plan on starting the assignment?*
Contact? *Who can I contact if I get stuck?*

Daily Planner

Week of	What am I working on? (Long-term goal)

Date: **MONDAY**	Date: **TUESDAY**	Date: **WEDNESDAY**
URGENT: REMEMBER THIS!	**URGENT: REMEMBER THIS!**	**URGENT: REMEMBER THIS!**

Subject	Due date	Subject	Due date	Subject	Due date

How long?	Start time?	How long?	Start time?	How long?	Start time?
Materials?		Materials?		Materials?	
Contact		Contact		Contact	

Subject	Due date	Subject	Due date	Subject	Due date

How long?	Start time?	How long?	Start time?	How long?	Start time?
Materials?		Materials?		Materials?	
Contact		Contact		Contact	

Subject	Due date	Subject	Due date	Subject	Due date

How long?	Start time?	How long?	Start time?	How long?	Start time?
Materials?		Materials?		Materials?	
Contact		Contact		Contact	

Subject	Due date	Subject	Due date	Subject	Due date

How long?	Start time?	How long?	Start time?	How long?	Start time?
Materials?		Materials?		Materials?	
Contact		Contact		Contact	

Daily reflection	Daily reflection	Daily reflection

Key to Questions

How long? *How long will the assignment take?*
Materials? *Do I have all the materials needed to complete the assignment?*

Start time? *When do I plan on starting the assignment?*
Contact? *Who can I contact if I get stuck?*

What am I working on? (Long-term goal)

_____

Date: **THURSDAY**	Date: **FRIDAY**	Dates: **SATURDAY** & **SUNDAY**
URGENT: REMEMBER THIS!	**URGENT: REMEMBER THIS!**	Weekend plans/activities
Subject / Due date	Subject / Due date	
How long? / Start time?	How long? / Start time?	
Materials?	Materials?	
Contact	Contact	
Subject / Due date	Subject / Due date	To-do list
How long? / Start time?	How long? / Start time?	
Materials?	Materials?	
Contact	Contact	
Subject / Due date	Subject / Due date	Saturday schedule
How long? / Start time?	How long? / Start time?	
Materials?	Materials?	
Contact	Contact	
Subject / Due date	Subject / Due date	Sunday schedule
How long? / Start time?	How long? / Start time?	
Materials?	Materials?	
Contact	Contact	
Daily reflection	Daily reflection	Weekend reflection

Key to Questions

How long? _How long will the assignment take?_ **Start time?** _When do I plan on starting_
Materials? _Do I have all the materials needed_   _the assignment?_
    to complete the assignment?   **Contact?** _Who can I contact if I get stuck?_

Things to Remember for Next Month

(e.g., upcoming projects; midterms, finals or major exams; start of sport season or other extracurricular activity; change in work schedule; family or class trips; school vacation)

Monthly Planner

December 2015

S	M	T	W	T	F	S
		1	2	3	4	5
6	7	8	9	10	11	12
13	14	15	16	17	18	19
20	21	22	23	24	25	26
27	28	29	30	31		

December 2016

S	M	T	W	T	F	S
				1	2	3
4	5	6	7	8	9	10
11	12	13	14	15	16	17
18	19	20	21	22	23	24
25	26	27	28	29	30	31

December 2017

S	M	T	W	T	F	S
					1	2
3	4	5	6	7	8	9
10	11	12	13	14	15	16
17	18	19	20	21	22	23
24	25	26	27	28	29	30
31						

My EXECUTIVE SKILL goal:

My ACADEMIC goal:

**Be sure to check off when you've finished each assignment.
When you hand it in, <u>cross it out</u>!**

Sunday	Monday	Tuesday	Wednesday	Thursday	Friday	Saturday

Daily Planner

<table>
<tr><td>Week of</td><td>What am I working on? (Long-term goal)</td></tr>
</table>

Date: **MONDAY**	Date: **TUESDAY**	Date: **WEDNESDAY**
URGENT: REMEMBER THIS!	URGENT: REMEMBER THIS!	URGENT: REMEMBER THIS!
Subject — Due date	Subject — Due date	Subject — Due date
How long? — Start time?	How long? — Start time?	How long? — Start time?
Materials?	Materials?	Materials?
Contact	Contact	Contact
Subject — Due date	Subject — Due date	Subject — Due date
How long? — Start time?	How long? — Start time?	How long? — Start time?
Materials?	Materials?	Materials?
Contact	Contact	Contact
Subject — Due date	Subject — Due date	Subject — Due date
How long? — Start time?	How long? — Start time?	How long? — Start time?
Materials?	Materials?	Materials?
Contact	Contact	Contact
Subject — Due date	Subject — Due date	Subject — Due date
How long? — Start time?	How long? — Start time?	How long? — Start time?
Materials?	Materials?	Materials?
Contact	Contact	Contact
Daily reflection	Daily reflection	Daily reflection

Key to Questions

How long? *How long will the assignment take?*
Materials? *Do I have all the materials needed to complete the assignment?*

Start time? *When do I plan on starting the assignment?*
Contact? *Who can I contact if I get stuck?*

What am I working on? (Long-term goal)

Date: **THURSDAY**		Date: **FRIDAY**		Dates: **SATURDAY** & **SUNDAY**
URGENT: REMEMBER THIS!		**URGENT: REMEMBER THIS!**		Weekend plans/activities
Subject	Due date	Subject	Due date	
How long?	Start time?	How long?	Start time?	
Materials?		Materials?		
Contact		Contact		
Subject	Due date	Subject	Due date	To-do list
How long?	Start time?	How long?	Start time?	
Materials?		Materials?		
Contact		Contact		
Subject	Due date	Subject	Due date	Saturday schedule
How long?	Start time?	How long?	Start time?	
Materials?		Materials?		
Contact		Contact		
Subject	Due date	Subject	Due date	Sunday schedule
How long?	Start time?	How long?	Start time?	
Materials?		Materials?		
Contact		Contact		
Daily reflection		Daily reflection		Weekend reflection

Key to Questions

How long? *How long will the assignment take?*
Materials? *Do I have all the materials needed to complete the assignment?*

Start time? *When do I plan on starting the assignment?*
Contact? *Who can I contact if I get stuck?*

Daily Planner

Week of	What am I working on? (Long-term goal)

Date: **MONDAY**	Date: **TUESDAY**	Date: **WEDNESDAY**
URGENT: REMEMBER THIS!	**URGENT: REMEMBER THIS!**	**URGENT: REMEMBER THIS!**

Subject	Due date	Subject	Due date	Subject	Due date

How long?	Start time?	How long?	Start time?	How long?	Start time?
Materials?		Materials?		Materials?	
Contact		Contact		Contact	

Subject	Due date	Subject	Due date	Subject	Due date

How long?	Start time?	How long?	Start time?	How long?	Start time?
Materials?		Materials?		Materials?	
Contact		Contact		Contact	

Subject	Due date	Subject	Due date	Subject	Due date

How long?	Start time?	How long?	Start time?	How long?	Start time?
Materials?		Materials?		Materials?	
Contact		Contact		Contact	

Subject	Due date	Subject	Due date	Subject	Due date

How long?	Start time?	How long?	Start time?	How long?	Start time?
Materials?		Materials?		Materials?	
Contact		Contact		Contact	

Daily reflection	Daily reflection	Daily reflection

Key to Questions

How long? *How long will the assignment take?*
Materials? *Do I have all the materials needed to complete the assignment?*

Start time? *When do I plan on starting the assignment?*
Contact? *Who can I contact if I get stuck?*

What am I working on? (Long-term goal)

Date: **THURSDAY**		Date: **FRIDAY**		Dates: **SATURDAY** & **SUNDAY**
URGENT: REMEMBER THIS!		**URGENT: REMEMBER THIS!**		Weekend plans/activities
Subject	Due date	Subject	Due date	
How long?	Start time?	How long?	Start time?	
Materials?		Materials?		
Contact		Contact		
Subject	Due date	Subject	Due date	To-do list
How long?	Start time?	How long?	Start time?	
Materials?		Materials?		
Contact		Contact		
Subject	Due date	Subject	Due date	Saturday schedule
How long?	Start time?	How long?	Start time?	
Materials?		Materlals?		
Contact		Contact		
Subject	Due date	Subject	Due date	Sunday schedule
How long?	Start time?	How long?	Start time?	
Materials?		Materials?		
Contact		Contact		
Daily reflection		Daily reflection		Weekend reflection

Key to Questions

How long? *How long will the assignment take?*
Materials? *Do I have all the materials needed to complete the assignment?*

Start time? *When do I plan on starting the assignment?*
Contact? *Who can I contact if I get stuck?*

Daily Planner

Week of	What am I working on? (Long-term goal)

Date: **MONDAY**	Date: **TUESDAY**	Date: **WEDNESDAY**
URGENT: REMEMBER THIS!	**URGENT: REMEMBER THIS!**	**URGENT: REMEMBER THIS!**

Subject	Due date	Subject	Due date	Subject	Due date

How long?	Start time?	How long?	Start time?	How long?	Start time?
Materials?		Materials?		Materials?	
Contact		Contact		Contact	

Subject	Due date	Subject	Due date	Subject	Due date

How long?	Start time?	How long?	Start time?	How long?	Start time?
Materials?		Materials?		Materials?	
Contact		Contact		Contact	

Subject	Due date	Subject	Due date	Subject	Due date

How long?	Start time?	How long?	Start time?	How long?	Start time?
Materials?		Materials?		Materials?	
Contact		Contact		Contact	

Subject	Due date	Subject	Due date	Subject	Due date

How long?	Start time?	How long?	Start time?	How long?	Start time?
Materials?		Materials?		Materials?	
Contact		Contact		Contact	

Daily reflection	Daily reflection	Daily reflection

Key to Questions

How long? *How long will the assignment take?*
Materials? *Do I have all the materials needed to complete the assignment?*

Start time? *When do I plan on starting the assignment?*
Contact? *Who can I contact if I get stuck?*

What am I working on? (Long-term goal)

Date: **THURSDAY**		Date: **FRIDAY**		Dates: **SATURDAY & SUNDAY**
URGENT: REMEMBER THIS!		**URGENT: REMEMBER THIS!**		Weekend plans/activities
Subject	Due date	Subject	Due date	
How long?	Start time?	How long?	Start time?	
Materials?		Materials?		
Contact		Contact		
Subject	Due date	Subject	Due date	To-do list
How long?	Start time?	How long?	Start time?	
Materials?		Materials?		
Contact		Contact		
Subject	Due date	Subject	Due date	Saturday schedule
How long?	Start time?	How long?	Start time?	
Materials?		Materials?		
Contact		Contact		
Subject	Due date	Subject	Due date	Sunday schedule
How long?	Start time?	I low long?	Start time?	
Materials?		Materials?		
Contact		Contact		
Daily reflection		Daily reflection		Weekend reflection

Key to Questions

How long? *How long will the assignment take?*
Materials? *Do I have all the materials needed to complete the assignment?*

Start time? *When do I plan on starting the assignment?*
Contact? *Who can I contact if I get stuck?*

Daily Planner

Week of
_____

What am I working on? (Long-term goal)
_____

Date: **MONDAY**	Date: **TUESDAY**	Date: **WEDNESDAY**
URGENT: REMEMBER THIS!	**URGENT: REMEMBER THIS!**	**URGENT: REMEMBER THIS!**

Subject	Due date	Subject	Due date	Subject	Due date

How long?	Start time?	How long?	Start time?	How long?	Start time?
Materials?		Materials?		Materials?	
Contact		Contact		Contact	

Subject	Due date	Subject	Due date	Subject	Due date

How long?	Start time?	How long?	Start time?	How long?	Start time?
Materials?		Materials?		Materials?	
Contact		Contact		Contact	

Subject	Due date	Subject	Due date	Subject	Due date

How long?	Start time?	How long?	Start time?	How long?	Start time?
Materials?		Materials?		Materials?	
Contact		Contact		Contact	

Subject	Due date	Subject	Due date	Subject	Due date

How long?	Start time?	How long?	Start time?	How long?	Start time?
Materials?		Materials?		Materials?	
Contact		Contact		Contact	

Daily reflection	Daily reflection	Daily reflection

Key to Questions

How long? *How long will the assignment take?*

Materials? *Do I have all the materials needed to complete the assignment?*

Start time? *When do I plan on starting the assignment?*

Contact? *Who can I contact if I get stuck?*

What am I working on? (Long-term goal)

Date: **THURSDAY**		Date: **FRIDAY**		Dates: **SATURDAY** & **SUNDAY**
URGENT: REMEMBER THIS!		**URGENT: REMEMBER THIS!**		Weekend plans/activities
Subject	Due date	Subject	Due date	
How long?	Start time?	How long?	Start time?	
Materials?		Materials?		
Contact		Contact		
Subject	Due date	Subject	Due date	To-do list
How long?	Start time?	How long?	Start time?	
Materials?		Materials?		
Contact		Contact		
Subject	Due date	Subject	Due date	Saturday schedule
How long?	Start time?	How long?	Start time?	
Materials?		Materials?		
Contact		Contact		
Subject	Due date	Subject	Due date	Sunday schedule
How long?	Start time?	How long?	Start time?	
Materials?		Materials?		
Contact		Contact		
Daily reflection		Daily reflection		Weekend reflection

Key to Questions

How long? *How long will the assignment take?*   **Start time?** *When do I plan on starting*
Materials? *Do I have all the materials needed*   *the assignment?*
to complete the assignment?   **Contact?** *Who can I contact if I get stuck?*

Things to Remember for Next Month

(e.g., upcoming projects; midterms, finals or major exams; start of sport season or other extracurricular activity; change in work schedule; family or class trips; school vacation)

Monthly Planner

January 2016

S	M	T	W	T	F	S
					1	2
3	4	5	6	7	8	9
10	11	12	13	14	15	16
17	18	19	20	21	22	23
24	25	26	27	28	29	30
31						

January 2017

S	M	T	W	T	F	S
1	2	3	4	5	6	7
8	9	10	11	12	13	14
15	16	17	18	19	20	21
22	23	24	25	26	27	28
29	30	31				

January 2018

S	M	T	W	T	F	S
	1	2	3	4	5	6
7	8	9	10	11	12	13
14	15	16	17	18	19	20
21	22	23	24	25	26	27
28	29	30	31			

My EXECUTIVE SKILL goal:

My ACADEMIC goal:

**Be sure to check off when you've finished each assignment.
When you hand it in, <u>cross it out</u>!**

Sunday	Monday	Tuesday	Wednesday	Thursday	Friday	Saturday

Daily Planner

Week of
_____

What am I working on? (Long-term goal)
_____

Date: **MONDAY**	Date: **TUESDAY**	Date: **WEDNESDAY**
URGENT: REMEMBER THIS!	**URGENT: REMEMBER THIS!**	**URGENT: REMEMBER THIS!**

Subject	Due date	Subject	Due date	Subject	Due date
How long?	Start time?	How long?	Start time?	How long?	Start time?
Materials?		Materials?		Materials?	
Contact		Contact		Contact	

Subject	Due date	Subject	Due date	Subject	Due date
How long?	Start time?	How long?	Start time?	How long?	Start time?
Materials?		Materials?		Materials?	
Contact		Contact		Contact	

Subject	Due date	Subject	Due date	Subject	Due date
How long?	Start time?	How long?	Start time?	How long?	Start time?
Materials?		Materials?		Materials?	
Contact		Contact		Contact	

Subject	Due date	Subject	Due date	Subject	Due date
How long?	Start time?	How long?	Start time?	How long?	Start time?
Materials?		Materials?		Materials?	
Contact		Contact		Contact	

Daily reflection	Daily reflection	Daily reflection

Key to Questions

How long? _How long will the assignment take?_   **Start time?** _When do I plan on starting_
Materials? _Do I have all the materials needed_   _the assignment?_
     to complete the assignment?   **Contact?** _Who can I contact if I get stuck?_

What am I working on? (Long-term goal)

Date: **THURSDAY**	Date: **FRIDAY**	Dates: **SATURDAY** & **SUNDAY**
URGENT: REMEMBER THIS!	**URGENT: REMEMBER THIS!**	Weekend plans/activities
Subject — Due date	Subject — Due date	
How long? — Start time? Materials? Contact	How long? — Start time? Materials? Contact	
Subject — Due date	Subject — Due date	To-do list
How long? — Start time? Materials? Contact	How long? — Start time? Materials? Contact	
Subject — Due date	Subject — Due date	Saturday schedule
How long? — Start time? Materials? Contact	How long? — Start time? Materials? Contact	
Subject — Due date	Subject — Due date	Sunday schedule
How long? — Start time? Materials? Contact	How long? — Start time? Materials? Contact	
Daily reflection	Daily reflection	Weekend reflection

Key to Questions

How long? *How long will the assignment take?*
Materials? *Do I have all the materials needed to complete the assignment?*

Start time? *When do I plan on starting the assignment?*
Contact? *Who can I contact if I get stuck?*

Daily Planner

Week of	What am I working on? (Long-term goal)

Date: **MONDAY**	Date: **TUESDAY**	Date: **WEDNESDAY**
URGENT: REMEMBER THIS!	**URGENT: REMEMBER THIS!**	**URGENT: REMEMBER THIS!**

Subject — Due date	Subject — Due date	Subject — Due date
How long? — Start time?	How long? — Start time?	How long? — Start time?
Materials?	Materials?	Materials?
Contact	Contact	Contact
Subject — Due date	Subject — Due date	Subject — Due date
How long? — Start time?	How long? — Start time?	How long? — Start time?
Materials?	Materials?	Materials?
Contact	Contact	Contact
Subject — Due date	Subject — Due date	Subject — Due date
How long? — Start time?	How long? — Start time?	How long? — Start time?
Materials?	Materials?	Materials?
Contact	Contact	Contact
Subject — Due date	Subject — Due date	Subject — Due date
How long? — Start time?	How long? — Start time?	How long? — Start time?
Materials?	Materials?	Materials?
Contact	Contact	Contact
Daily reflection	Daily reflection	Daily reflection

Key to Questions

How long? *How long will the assignment take?*   **Start time?** *When do I plan on starting the assignment?*
Materials? *Do I have all the materials needed to complete the assignment?*   **Contact?** *Who can I contact if I get stuck?*

What am I working on? (Long-term goal)

Date: **THURSDAY**		Date: **FRIDAY**		Dates: **SATURDAY** & **SUNDAY**
URGENT: REMEMBER THIS!		URGENT: REMEMBER THIS!		Weekend plans/activities
Subject	Due date	Subject	Due date	
How long?	Start time?	How long?	Start time?	
Materials?		Materials?		
Contact		Contact		
Subject	Due date	Subject	Due date	To-do list
How long?	Start time?	How long?	Start time?	
Materials?		Materials?		
Contact		Contact		
Subject	Due date	Subject	Due date	Saturday schedule
How long?	Start time?	How long?	Start time?	
Materials?		Materials?		
Contact		Contact		
Subject	Due date	Subject	Due date	Sunday schedule
How long?	Start time?	How long?	Start time?	
Materials?		Materials?		
Contact		Contact		
Daily reflection		Daily reflection		Weekend reflection

Key to Questions

How long? *How long will the assignment take?*
Materials? *Do I have all the materials needed to complete the assignment?*

Start time? *When do I plan on starting the assignment?*
Contact? *Who can I contact if I get stuck?*

Daily Planner

Week of	What am I working on? (Long-term goal)

Date: **MONDAY**	Date: **TUESDAY**	Date: **WEDNESDAY**
URGENT: REMEMBER THIS!	**URGENT: REMEMBER THIS!**	**URGENT: REMEMBER THIS!**
Subject / Due date	Subject / Due date	Subject / Due date
How long? / Start time?	How long? / Start time?	How long? / Start time?
Materials?	Materials?	Materials?
Contact	Contact	Contact
Subject / Due date	Subject / Due date	Subject / Due date
How long? / Start time?	How long? / Start time?	How long? / Start time?
Materials?	Materials?	Materials?
Contact	Contact	Contact
Subject / Due date	Subject / Due date	Subject / Due date
How long? / Start time?	How long? / Start time?	How long? / Start time?
Materials?	Materials?	Materials?
Contact	Contact	Contact
Subject / Due date	Subject / Due date	Subject / Due date
How long? / Start time?	How long? / Start time?	How long? / Start time?
Materials?	Materials?	Materials?
Contact	Contact	Contact
Daily reflection	Daily reflection	Daily reflection

Key to Questions

How long? *How long will the assignment take?*

Materials? *Do I have all the materials needed to complete the assignment?*

Start time? *When do I plan on starting the assignment?*

Contact? *Who can I contact if I get stuck?*

What am I working on? (Long-term goal)

_____

Date: **THURSDAY**	Date: **FRIDAY**	Dates: **SATURDAY** & **SUNDAY**
URGENT: REMEMBER THIS!	**URGENT: REMEMBER THIS!**	Weekend plans/activities
Subject _____ Due date	Subject _____ Due date	
How long? _____ Start time?	How long? _____ Start time?	
Materials?	Materials?	
Contact	Contact	
Subject _____ Due date	Subject _____ Due date	To-do list
How long? _____ Start time?	How long? _____ Start time?	
Materials?	Materials?	
Contact	Contact	
Subject _____ Due date	Subject _____ Due date	Saturday schedule
How long? _____ Start time?	How long? _____ Start time?	
Materials?	Materials?	
Contact	Contact	
Subject _____ Due date	Subject _____ Due date	Sunday schedule
How long? _____ Start time?	How long? _____ Start time?	
Materials?	Materials?	
Contact	Contact	
Daily reflection	Daily reflection	Weekend reflection

Key to Questions

How long? _How long will the assignment take?_
Materials? _Do I have all the materials needed to complete the assignment?_

Start time? _When do I plan on starting the assignment?_
Contact? _Who can I contact if I get stuck?_

Daily Planner

Week of _____

What am I working on? (Long-term goal) _____

Date: **MONDAY**	Date: **TUESDAY**	Date: **WEDNESDAY**
URGENT: REMEMBER THIS!	**URGENT: REMEMBER THIS!**	**URGENT: REMEMBER THIS!**

Subject	Due date	Subject	Due date	Subject	Due date
How long?	Start time?	How long?	Start time?	How long?	Start time?
Materials?		Materials?		Materials?	
Contact		Contact		Contact	

Subject	Due date	Subject	Due date	Subject	Due date
How long?	Start time?	How long?	Start time?	How long?	Start time?
Materials?		Materials?		Materials?	
Contact		Contact		Contact	

Subject	Due date	Subject	Due date	Subject	Due date
How long?	Start time?	How long?	Start time?	How long?	Start tlme?
Materials?		Materials?		Materials?	
Contact		Contact		Contact	

Subject	Due date	Subject	Due date	Subject	Due date
How long?	Start time?	How long?	Start time?	How long?	Start time?
Materials?		Materials?		Materials?	
Contact		Contact		Contact	

Daily reflection	Daily reflection	Daily reflection

Key to Questions

How long? *How long will the assignment take?*

Materials? *Do I have all the materials needed to complete the assignment?*

Start time? *When do I plan on starting the assignment?*

Contact? *Who can I contact if I get stuck?*

What am I working on? (Long-term goal)

Date: **THURSDAY**		Date: **FRIDAY**		Dates: **SATURDAY** & **SUNDAY**
URGENT: REMEMBER THIS!		**URGENT: REMEMBER THIS!**		Weekend plans/activities
Subject	Due date	Subject	Due date	
How long?	Start time?	How long?	Start time?	
Materials?		Materials?		
Contact		Contact		
Subject	Due date	Subject	Due date	To-do list
How long?	Start time?	How long?	Start time?	
Materials?		Materials?		
Contact		Contact		
Subject	Due date	Subject	Due date	Saturday schedule
How long?	Start time?	How long?	Start time?	
Materials?		Materials?		
Contact		Contact		
Subject	Due date	Subject	Due date	Sunday schedule
How long?	Start time?	How long?	Start time?	
Materials?		Materials?		
Contact		Contact		
Daily reflection		Daily reflection		Weekend reflection

Key to Questions

How long? *How long will the assignment take?*   **Start time?** *When do I plan on starting the assignment?*

Materials? *Do I have all the materials needed to complete the assignment?*   **Contact?** *Who can I contact if I get stuck?*

Daily Planner

Week of

What am I working on? (Long-term goal)

Date: **MONDAY**	Date: **TUESDAY**	Date: **WEDNESDAY**
URGENT: REMEMBER THIS!	**URGENT: REMEMBER THIS!**	**URGENT: REMEMBER THIS!**

Subject	Due date	Subject	Due date	Subject	Due date
How long?	Start time?	How long?	Start time?	How long?	Start time?
Materials?		Materials?		Materials?	
Contact		Contact		Contact	

Subject	Due date	Subject	Due date	Subject	Due date
How long?	Start time?	How long?	Start time?	How long?	Start time?
Materials?		Materials?		Materials?	
Contact		Contact		Contact	

Subject	Due date	Subject	Due date	Subject	Due date
How long?	Start time?	How long?	Start time?	How long?	Start time?
Materials?		Materials?		Materials?	
Contact		Contact		Contact	

Subject	Due date	Subject	Due date	Subject	Due date
How long?	Start time?	How long?	Start time?	How long?	Start time?
Materials?		Materials?		Materials?	
Contact		Contact		Contact	

Daily reflection	Daily reflection	Daily reflection

Key to Questions

How long? *How long will the assignment take?*

Materials? *Do I have all the materials needed to complete the assignment?*

Start time? *When do I plan on starting the assignment?*

Contact? *Who can I contact if I get stuck?*

What am I working on? (Long-term goal)

Date: **THURSDAY**	Date: **FRIDAY**	Dates: **SATURDAY** & **SUNDAY**
URGENT: REMEMBER THIS!	**URGENT: REMEMBER THIS!**	Weekend plans/activities
Subject — Due date	Subject — Due date	
How long? — Start time? Materials? Contact	How long? — Start time? Materials? Contact	
Subject — Due date	Subject — Due date	To-do list
How long? — Start time? Materials? Contact	How long? — Start time? Materials? Contact	
Subject — Due date	Subject — Due date	Saturday schedule
How long? — Start time? Materials? Contact	How long? — Start time? Materials? Contact	
Subject — Due date	Subject — Due date	Sunday schedule
How long? — Start time? Materials? Contact	How long? — Start time? Materials? Contact	
Daily reflection	Daily reflection	Weekend reflection

Key to Questions

How long? *How long will the assignment take?*   **Start time?** *When do I plan on starting the assignment?*

Materials? *Do I have all the materials needed to complete the assignment?*   **Contact?** *Who can I contact if I get stuck?*

Things to Remember for Next Month

(e.g., upcoming projects; midterms, finals or major exams; start of sport season or other extracurricular activity; change in work schedule; family or class trips; school vacation)

Monthly Planner

February 2016

S	M	T	W	T	F	S
	1	2	3	4	5	6
7	8	9	10	11	12	13
14	15	16	17	18	19	20
21	22	23	24	25	26	27
28	29					

February 2017

S	M	T	W	T	F	S
			1	2	3	4
5	6	7	8	9	10	11
12	13	14	15	16	17	18
19	20	21	22	23	24	25
26	27	28				

February 2018

S	M	T	W	T	F	S
				1	2	3
4	5	6	7	8	9	10
11	12	13	14	15	16	17
18	19	20	21	22	23	24
25	26	27	28			

My EXECUTIVE SKILL goal:

My ACADEMIC goal:

**Be sure to check off when you've finished each assignment.
When you hand it in, cross it out!**

Sunday	Monday	Tuesday	Wednesday	Thursday	Friday	Saturday

93

Daily Planner

Week of	What am I working on? (Long-term goal)

Date: **MONDAY**	Date: **TUESDAY**	Date: **WEDNESDAY**
URGENT: REMEMBER THIS!	URGENT: REMEMBER THIS!	URGENT: REMEMBER THIS!

Subject	Due date	Subject	Due date	Subject	Due date
How long?	Start time?	How long?	Start time?	How long?	Start time?
Materials?		Materials?		Materials?	
Contact		Contact		Contact	

Subject	Due date	Subject	Due date	Subject	Due date
How long?	Start time?	How long?	Start time?	How long?	Start time?
Materials?		Materials?		Materials?	
Contact		Contact		Contact	

Subject	Due date	Subject	Due date	Subject	Due date
How long?	Start time?	How long?	Start time?	How long?	Start time?
Materials?		Materials?		Materials?	
Contact		Contact		Contact	

Subject	Due date	Subject	Due date	Subject	Due date
How long?	Start time?	How long?	Start time?	How long?	Start time?
Materials?		Materials?		Materials?	
Contact		Contact		Contact	

Daily reflection	Daily reflection	Daily reflection

Key to Questions

How long? *How long will the assignment take?*
Materials? *Do I have all the materials needed to complete the assignment?*

Start time? *When do I plan on starting the assignment?*
Contact? *Who can I contact if I get stuck?*

What am I working on? (Long-term goal)

_____

Date: **THURSDAY**	Date: **FRIDAY**	Dates: **SATURDAY** & **SUNDAY**
URGENT: REMEMBER THIS!	**URGENT: REMEMBER THIS!**	Weekend plans/activities
Subject / Due date	Subject / Due date	
How long? / Start time? Materials? Contact	How long? / Start time? Materials? Contact	
Subject / Due date	Subject / Due date	To-do list
How long? / Start time? Materials? Contact	How long? / Start time? Materials? Contact	
Subject / Due date	Subject / Due date	Saturday schedule
How long? / Start time? Materials? Contact	How long? / Start time? Materials? Contact	
Subject / Due date	Subject / Due date	Sunday schedule
How long? / Start time? Materials? Contact	How long? / Start time? Materials? Contact	
Daily reflection	Daily reflection	Weekend reflection

Key to Questions

How long? _How long will the assignment take?_   **Start time?** _When do I plan on starting_
Materials? _Do I have all the materials needed_   _the assignment?_
to complete the assignment?   **Contact?** _Who can I contact if I get stuck?_

Daily Planner

Week of	What am I working on? (Long-term goal)

Date: **MONDAY**	Date: **TUESDAY**	Date: **WEDNESDAY**
URGENT: REMEMBER THIS!	**URGENT: REMEMBER THIS!**	**URGENT: REMEMBER THIS!**

Subject	Due date	Subject	Due date	Subject	Due date

How long?	Start time?	How long?	Start time?	How long?	Start time?
Materials?		Materials?		Materials?	
Contact		Contact		Contact	

Subject	Due date	Subject	Due date	Subject	Due date

How long?	Start time?	How long?	Start time?	How long?	Start time?
Materials?		Materials?		Materials?	
Contact		Contact		Contact	

Subject	Due date	Subject	Due date	Subject	Due date

How long?	Start time?	How long?	Start time?	How long?	Start time?
Materials?		Materials?		Materials?	
Contact		Contact		Contact	

Subject	Due date	Subject	Due date	Subject	Due date

How long?	Start time?	How long?	Start time?	How long?	Start time?
Materials?		Materials?		Materials?	
Contact		Contact		Contact	

Daily reflection	Daily reflection	Daily reflection

Key to Questions

How long? *How long will the assignment take?*
Materials? *Do I have all the materials needed to complete the assignment?*

Start time? *When do I plan on starting the assignment?*
Contact? *Who can I contact if I get stuck?*

What am I working on? (Long-term goal)

Date: **THURSDAY**		Date: **FRIDAY**		Dates: **SATURDAY** & **SUNDAY**
URGENT: REMEMBER THIS!		**URGENT: REMEMBER THIS!**		Weekend plans/activities
Subject	Due date	Subject	Due date	
How long?	Start time?	How long?	Start time?	
Materials?		Materials?		
Contact		Contact		
Subject	Due date	Subject	Due date	To-do list
How long?	Start time?	How long?	Start time?	
Materials?		Materials?		
Contact		Contact		
Subject	Due date	Subject	Due date	Saturday schedule
How long?	Start time?	How long?	Start time?	
Materials?		Materials?		
Contact		Contact		
Subject	Due date	Subject	Due date	Sunday schedule
How long?	Start time?	How long?	Start time?	
Materials?		Materials?		
Contact		Contact		
Daily reflection		Daily reflection		Weekend reflection

Key to Questions

How long? *How long will the assignment take?* **Start time?** *When do I plan on starting*
Materials? *Do I have all the materials needed*   *the assignment?*
to complete the assignment? **Contact?** *Who can I contact if I get stuck?*

Daily Planner

Week of	What am I working on? (Long-term goal)

_____

Date: **MONDAY**	Date: **TUESDAY**	Date: **WEDNESDAY**
URGENT: REMEMBER THIS!	**URGENT: REMEMBER THIS!**	**URGENT: REMEMBER THIS!**

Subject	Due date		Subject	Due date		Subject	Due date
How long?	Start time?		How long?	Start time?		How long?	Start time?
Materials?			Materials?			Materials?	
Contact			Contact			Contact	

Subject	Due date		Subject	Due date		Subject	Due date
How long?	Start time?		How long?	Start time?		How long?	Start time?
Materials?			Materials?			Materials?	
Contact			Contact			Contact	

Subject	Due date		Subject	Due date		Subject	Due date
How long?	Start time?		How long?	Start time?		How long?	Start time?
Materials?			Materials?			Materials?	
Contact			Contact			Contact	

Subject	Due date		Subject	Due date		Subject	Due date
How long?	Start time?		How long?	Start time?		How long?	Start time?
Materials?			Materials?			Materials?	
Contact			Contact			Contact	

Daily reflection	Daily reflection	Daily reflection

Key to Questions

How long? _How long will the assignment take?_
Materials? _Do I have all the materials needed to complete the assignment?_

Start time? _When do I plan on starting the assignment?_
Contact? _Who can I contact if I get stuck?_

What am I working on? (Long-term goal)

_____

Date: **THURSDAY**	Date: **FRIDAY**	Dates: **SATURDAY** & **SUNDAY**
URGENT: REMEMBER THIS!	**URGENT: REMEMBER THIS!**	Weekend plans/activities
Subject / Due date	Subject / Due date	
How long? / Start time?	How long? / Start time?	
Materials?	Materials?	
Contact	Contact	
Subject / Due date	Subject / Due date	To-do list
How long? / Start time?	How long? / Start time?	
Materials?	Materials?	
Contact	Contact	
Subject / Due date	Subject / Due date	Saturday schedule
How long? / Start time?	How long? / Start time?	
Materials?	Materials?	
Contact	Contact	
Subject / Due date	Subject / Due date	Sunday schedule
How long? / Start time?	How long? / Start time?	
Materials?	Materials?	
Contact	Contact	
Daily reflection	Daily reflection	Weekend reflection

Key to Questions

How long? _How long will the assignment take?_   **Start time?** _When do I plan on starting_
Materials? _Do I have all the materials needed_   _the assignment?_
     to complete the assignment?   **Contact?** _Who can I contact if I get stuck?_

Daily Planner

Week of	What am I working on? (Long-term goal)
_____	_____

Date: **MONDAY**	Date: **TUESDAY**	Date: **WEDNESDAY**
URGENT: REMEMBER THIS!	**URGENT: REMEMBER THIS!**	**URGENT: REMEMBER THIS!**

Subject	Due date	Subject	Due date	Subject	Due date
How long?	Start time?	How long?	Start time?	How long?	Start time?
Materials?		Materials?		Materials?	
Contact		Contact		Contact	

Subject	Due date	Subject	Due date	Subject	Due date
How long?	Start time?	How long?	Start time?	How long?	Start time?
Materials?		Materials?		Materials?	
Contact		Contact		Contact	

Subject	Due date	Subject	Due date	Subject	Due date
How long?	Start time?	How long?	Start time?	How long?	Start time?
Materials?		Materials?		Materials?	
Contact		Contact		Contact	

Subject	Due date	Subject	Due date	Subject	Due date
How long?	Start time?	How long?	Start time?	How long?	Start time?
Materials?		Materials?		Materials?	
Contact		Contact		Contact	

Daily reflection	Daily reflection	Daily reflection

Key to Questions

How long? *How long will the assignment take?*

Materials? *Do I have all the materials needed to complete the assignment?*

Start time? *When do I plan on starting the assignment?*

Contact? *Who can I contact if I get stuck?*

What am I working on? (Long-term goal)

Date: **THURSDAY**		Date: **FRIDAY**		Dates: **SATURDAY** & **SUNDAY**
URGENT: REMEMBER THIS!		**URGENT: REMEMBER THIS!**		Weekend plans/activities
Subject	Due date	Subject	Due date	
How long?	Start time?	How long?	Start time?	
Materials?		Materials?		
Contact		Contact		
Subject	Due date	Subject	Due date	To-do list
How long?	Start time?	How long?	Start time?	
Materials?		Materials?		
Contact		Contact		
Subject	Due date	Subject	Due date	Saturday schedule
How long?	Start time?	How long?	Start time?	
Materials?		Materials?		
Contact		Contact		
Subject	Due date	Subject	Due date	Sunday schedule
How long?	Start time?	How long?	Start time?	
Materials?		Materials?		
Contact		Contact		
Daily reflection		Daily reflection		Weekend reflection

Key to Questions

How long? *How long will the assignment take?*   **Start time?** *When do I plan on starting*
Materials? *Do I have all the materials needed*   *the assignment?*
    to complete the assignment?   **Contact?** *Who can I contact if I get stuck?*

Things to Remember for Next Month

(e.g., upcoming projects; midterms, finals or major exams; start of sport season or other extracurricular activity; change in work schedule; family or class trips; school vacation)

Monthly Planner

MARCH

March 2016

S	M	T	W	T	F	S
		1	2	3	4	5
6	7	8	9	10	11	12
13	14	15	16	17	18	19
20	21	22	23	24	25	26
27	28	29	30	31		

March 2017

S	M	T	W	T	F	S
			1	2	3	4
5	6	7	8	9	10	11
12	13	14	15	16	17	18
19	20	21	22	23	24	25
26	27	28	29	30	31	

March 2018

S	M	T	W	T	F	S
				1	2	3
4	5	6	7	8	9	10
11	12	13	14	15	16	17
18	19	20	21	22	23	24
25	26	27	28	29	30	31

My EXECUTIVE SKILL goal:

My ACADEMIC goal:

Be sure to check off when you've finished each assignment.
When you hand it in, cross it out!

Sunday	Monday	Tuesday	Wednesday	Thursday	Friday	Saturday

Daily Planner

Week of

_____

What am I working on? (Long-term goal)

_____

Date: **MONDAY**	Date: **TUESDAY**	Date: **WEDNESDAY**
URGENT: REMEMBER THIS!	**URGENT: REMEMBER THIS!**	**URGENT: REMEMBER THIS!**

Subject	Due date	Subject	Due date	Subject	Due date

How long?	Start time?	How long?	Start time?	How long?	Start time?
Materials?		Materials?		Materials?	
Contact		Contact		Contact	

Subject	Due date	Subject	Due date	Subject	Due date

How long?	Start time?	How long?	Start time?	How long?	Start time?
Materials?		Materials?		Materials?	
Contact		Contact		Contact	

Subject	Due date	Subject	Due date	Subject	Due date

How long?	Start time?	How long?	Start time?	How long?	Start time?
Materials?		Materials?		Materials?	
Contact		Contact		Contact	

Subject	Due date	Subject	Due date	Subject	Due date

How long?	Start time?	How long?	Start time?	How long?	Start time?
Materials?		Materials?		Materials?	
Contact		Contact		Contact	

Daily reflection	Daily reflection	Daily reflection

Key to Questions

How long? _How long will the assignment take?_

Materials? _Do I have all the materials needed to complete the assignment?_

Start time? _When do I plan on starting the assignment?_

Contact? _Who can I contact if I get stuck?_

What am I working on? (Long-term goal)

Date: **THURSDAY**		Date: **FRIDAY**		Dates: **SATURDAY** & **SUNDAY**
URGENT: REMEMBER THIS!		**URGENT: REMEMBER THIS!**		Weekend plans/activities
Subject	Due date	Subject	Due date	
How long?	Start time?	How long?	Start time?	
Materials?		Materials?		
Contact		Contact		
Subject	Due date	Subject	Due date	To-do list
How long?	Start time?	How long?	Start time?	
Materials?		Materials?		
Contact		Contact		
Subject	Due date	Subject	Due date	Saturday schedule
How long?	Start time?	How long?	Start time?	
Materials?		Materials?		
Contact		Contact		
Subject	Due date	Subject	Due date	Sunday schedule
How long?	Start time?	How long?	Start time?	
Materials?		Materials?		
Contact		Contact		
Daily reflection		Daily reflection		Weekend reflection

Key to Questions

How long? *How long will the assignment take?*
Materials? *Do I have all the materials needed to complete the assignment?*

Start time? *When do I plan on starting the assignment?*
Contact? *Who can I contact if I get stuck?*

Daily Planner

Week of
_____

What am I working on? (Long-term goal)
_____

Date: **MONDAY**	Date: **TUESDAY**	Date: **WEDNESDAY**
URGENT: REMEMBER THIS!	**URGENT: REMEMBER THIS!**	**URGENT: REMEMBER THIS!**

Subject	Due date	Subject	Due date	Subject	Due date

How long?	Start time?	How long?	Start time?	How long?	Start time?
Materials?		Materials?		Materials?	
Contact		Contact		Contact	

Subject	Due date	Subject	Due date	Subject	Due date

How long?	Start time?	How long?	Start time?	How long?	Start time?
Materials?		Materials?		Materials?	
Contact		Contact		Contact	

Subject	Due date	Subject	Due date	Subject	Due date

How long?	Start time?	How long?	Start time?	How long?	Start time?
Materials?		Materials?		Materials?	
Contact		Contact		Contact	

Subject	Due date	Subject	Due date	Subject	Due date

How long?	Start time?	How long?	Start time?	How long?	Start time?
Materials?		Materials?		Materials?	
Contact		Contact		Contact	

Daily reflection	Daily reflection	Daily reflection

Key to Questions

How long? *How long will the assignment take?*
Materials? *Do I have all the materials needed to complete the assignment?*

Start time? *When do I plan on starting the assignment?*
Contact? *Who can I contact if I get stuck?*

106

What am I working on? (Long-term goal)

Date: **THURSDAY**	Date: **FRIDAY**	Dates: **SATURDAY** & **SUNDAY**
URGENT: REMEMBER THIS!	**URGENT: REMEMBER THIS!**	Weekend plans/activities
Subject / Due date	Subject / Due date	
How long? / Start time?	How long? / Start time?	
Materials?	Materials?	
Contact	Contact	
Subject / Due date	Subject / Due date	To-do list
How long? / Start time?	How long? / Start time?	
Materials?	Materials?	
Contact	Contact	
Subject / Due date	Subject / Due date	Saturday schedule
How long? / Start time?	How long? / Start time?	
Materials?	Materials?	
Contact	Contact	
Subject / Due date	Subject / Due date	Sunday schedule
How long? / Start time?	How long? / Start time?	
Materials?	Materials?	
Contact	Contact	
Daily reflection	Daily reflection	Weekend reflection

Key to Questions

How long? *How long will the assignment take?*
Materials? *Do I have all the materials needed to complete the assignment?*
Start time? *When do I plan on starting the assignment?*
Contact? *Who can I contact if I get stuck?*

Daily Planner

Week of

What am I working on? (Long-term goal)

Date: **MONDAY**	Date: **TUESDAY**	Date: **WEDNESDAY**
URGENT: REMEMBER THIS!	URGENT: REMEMBER THIS!	URGENT: REMEMBER THIS!

Subject	Due date	Subject	Due date	Subject	Due date

How long?	Start time?	How long?	Start time?	How long?	Start time?
Materials?		Materials?		Materials?	
Contact		Contact		Contact	

Subject	Due date	Subject	Due date	Subject	Due date

How long?	Start time?	How long?	Start time?	How long?	Start time?
Materials?		Materials?		Materials?	
Contact		Contact		Contact	

Subject	Due date	Subject	Due date	Subject	Due date

How long?	Start time?	How long?	Start time?	How long?	Start time?
Materials?		Materials?		Materials?	
Contact		Contact		Contact	

Subject	Due date	Subject	Due date	Subject	Due date

How long?	Start time?	How long?	Start time?	How long?	Start time?
Materials?		Materials?		Materials?	
Contact		Contact		Contact	

Daily reflection	Daily reflection	Daily reflection

Key to Questions

How long? *How long will the assignment take?*
Materials? *Do I have all the materials needed to complete the assignment?*

Start time? *When do I plan on starting the assignment?*
Contact? *Who can I contact if I get stuck?*

What am I working on? (Long-term goal)

Date: **THURSDAY**		Date: **FRIDAY**		Dates: **SATURDAY & SUNDAY**
URGENT: REMEMBER THIS!		**URGENT: REMEMBER THIS!**		Weekend plans/activities
Subject	Due date	Subject	Due date	
How long?	Start time?	How long?	Start time?	
Materials?		Materials?		
Contact		Contact		
Subject	Due date	Subject	Due date	To-do list
How long?	Start time?	How long?	Start time?	
Materials?		Materials?		
Contact		Contact		
Subject	Due date	Subject	Due date	Saturday schedule
How long?	Start time?	How long?	Start time?	
Materials?		Materials?		
Contact		Contact		
Subject	Due date	Subject	Due date	Sunday schedule
How long?	Start time?	How long?	Start time?	
Materials?		Materials?		
Contact		Contact		
Daily reflection		Daily reflection		Weekend reflection

Key to Questions

How long? *How long will the assignment take?*
Materials? *Do I have all the materials needed to complete the assignment?*

Start time? *When do I plan on starting the assignment?*
Contact? *Who can I contact if I get stuck?*

Daily Planner

What am I working on? (Long-term goal)

Date: **MONDAY**	Date: **TUESDAY**	Date: **WEDNESDAY**
URGENT: REMEMBER THIS!	**URGENT: REMEMBER THIS!**	**URGENT: REMEMBER THIS!**

Subject	Due date	Subject	Due date	Subject	Due date

How long?	Start time?	How long?	Start time?	How long?	Start time?
Materials?		Materials?		Materials?	
Contact		Contact		Contact	

Subject	Due date	Subject	Due date	Subject	Due date

How long?	Start time?	How long?	Start time?	How long?	Start time?
Materials?		Materials?		Materials?	
Contact		Contact		Contact	

Subject	Due date	Subject	Due date	Subject	Due date

How long?	Start time?	How long?	Start time?	How long?	Start time?
Materials?		Materials?		Materials?	
Contact		Contact		Contact	

Subject	Due date	Subject	Due date	Subject	Due date

How long?	Start time?	How long?	Start time?	How long?	Start time?
Materials?		Materials?		Materials?	
Contact		Contact		Contact	

Daily reflection	Daily reflection	Daily reflection

Key to Questions

How long? *How long will the assignment take?*
Materials? *Do I have all the materials needed to complete the assignment?*

Start time? *When do I plan on starting the assignment?*
Contact? *Who can I contact if I get stuck?*

What am I working on? (Long-term goal)

Date: **THURSDAY**	Date: **FRIDAY**	Dates: **SATURDAY & SUNDAY**
URGENT: REMEMBER THIS!	URGENT: REMEMBER THIS!	Weekend plans/activities
Subject / Due date	Subject / Due date	
How long? / Start time?	How long? / Start time?	
Materials?	Materials?	
Contact	Contact	
Subject / Due date	Subject / Due date	To-do list
How long? / Start time?	How long? / Start time?	
Materials?	Materials?	
Contact	Contact	
Subject / Due date	Subject / Due date	Saturday schedule
How long? / Start time?	How long? / Start time?	
Materials?	Materials?	
Contact	Contact	
Subject / Due date	Subject / Due date	Sunday schedule
How long? / Start time?	How long? / Start time?	
Materials?	Materials?	
Contact	Contact	
Daily reflection	Daily reflection	Weekend reflection

Key to Questions

How long? *How long will the assignment take?*
Materials? *Do I have all the materials needed to complete the assignment?*

Start time? *When do I plan on starting the assignment?*
Contact? *Who can I contact if I get stuck?*

Daily Planner

Week of
_____

What am I working on? (Long-term goal)
_____

Date: **MONDAY**	Date: **TUESDAY**	Date: **WEDNESDAY**
URGENT: REMEMBER THIS!	**URGENT: REMEMBER THIS!**	**URGENT: REMEMBER THIS!**

Subject	Due date	Subject	Due date	Subject	Due date
How long?	Start time?	How long?	Start time?	How long?	Start time?
Materials?		Materials?		Materials?	
Contact		Contact		Contact	
Subject	Due date	Subject	Due date	Subject	Due date
How long?	Start time?	How long?	Start time?	How long?	Start time?
Materials?		Materials?		Materials?	
Contact		Contact		Contact	
Subject	Due date	Subject	Due date	Subject	Due date
How long?	Start time?	How long?	Start time?	How long?	Start time?
Materials?		Materials?		Materials?	
Contact		Contact		Contact	
Subject	Due date	Subject	Due date	Subject	Due date
How long?	Start time?	How long?	Start time?	How long?	Start time?
Materials?		Materials?		Materials?	
Contact		Contact		Contact	
Daily reflection		Daily reflection		Daily reflection	

Key to Questions

How long? _How long will the assignment take?_

Materials? _Do I have all the materials needed to complete the assignment?_

Start time? _When do I plan on starting the assignment?_

Contact? _Who can I contact if I get stuck?_

What am I working on? (Long-term goal)

_____

Date: **THURSDAY**	Date: **FRIDAY**	Dates: **SATURDAY & SUNDAY**
URGENT: REMEMBER THIS!	**URGENT: REMEMBER THIS!**	Weekend plans/activities
Subject / Due date	Subject / Due date	
How long? / Start time?	How long? / Start time?	
Materials?	Materials?	
Contact	Contact	
Subject / Due date	Subject / Due date	To-do list
How long? / Start time?	How long? / Start time?	
Materials?	Materials?	
Contact	Contact	
Subject / Due date	Subject / Due date	Saturday schedule
How long? / Start time?	How long? / Start time?	
Materials?	Materials?	
Contact	Contact	
Subject / Due date	Subject / Due date	Sunday schedule
How long? / Start time?	How long? / Start time?	
Materials?	Materials?	
Contact	Contact	
Daily reflection	Daily reflection	Weekend reflection

Key to Questions

How long? *How long will the assignment take?*
Materials? *Do I have all the materials needed to complete the assignment?*

Start time? *When do I plan on starting the assignment?*
Contact? *Who can I contact if I get stuck?*

Things to Remember for Next Month

(e.g., upcoming projects; midterms, finals or major exams; start of sport season or other extracurricular activity; change in work schedule; family or class trips; school vacation)

Monthly Planner

April 2016

S	M	T	W	T	F	S
					1	2
3	4	5	6	7	8	9
10	11	12	13	14	15	16
17	18	19	20	21	22	23
24	25	26	27	28	29	30

April 2017

S	M	T	W	T	F	S
						1
2	3	4	5	6	7	8
9	10	11	12	13	14	15
16	17	18	19	20	21	22
23	24	25	26	27	28	29
30						

April 2018

S	M	T	W	T	F	S
1	2	3	4	5	6	7
8	9	10	11	12	13	14
15	16	17	18	19	20	21
22	23	24	25	26	27	28
29	30					

My EXECUTIVE SKILL goal:

My ACADEMIC goal:

**Be sure to check off when you've finished each assignment.
When you hand it in, cross it out!**

Sunday	Monday	Tuesday	Wednesday	Thursday	Friday	Saturday

Daily Planner

Week of	What am I working on? (Long-term goal)

Date: **MONDAY**	Date: **TUESDAY**	Date: **WEDNESDAY**
URGENT: REMEMBER THIS!	**URGENT: REMEMBER THIS!**	**URGENT: REMEMBER THIS!**

Subject	Due date	Subject	Due date	Subject	Due date

How long?	Start time?	How long?	Start time?	How long?	Start time?
Materials?		Materials?		Materials?	
Contact		Contact		Contact	

Subject	Due date	Subject	Due date	Subject	Due date

How long?	Start time?	How long?	Start time?	How long?	Start time?
Materials?		Materials?		Materials?	
Contact		Contact		Contact	

Subject	Due date	Subject	Due date	Subject	Due date

How long?	Start time?	How long?	Start time?	How long?	Start time?
Materials?		Materials?		Materials?	
Contact		Contact		Contact	

Subject	Due date	Subject	Due date	Subject	Due date

How long?	Start time?	How long?	Start time?	How long?	Start time?
Materials?		Materials?		Materials?	
Contact		Contact		Contact	
Daily reflection		Daily reflection		Daily reflection	

Key to Questions

How long? *How long will the assignment take?*
Materials? *Do I have all the materials needed to complete the assignment?*

Start time? *When do I plan on starting the assignment?*
Contact? *Who can I contact if I get stuck?*

What am I working on? (Long-term goal)

Date: **THURSDAY**		Date: **FRIDAY**		Dates: **SATURDAY** & **SUNDAY**
URGENT: REMEMBER THIS!		**URGENT: REMEMBER THIS!**		Weekend plans/activities
Subject	Due date	Subject	Due date	
How long?	Start time?	How long?	Start time?	
Materials?		Materials?		
Contact		Contact		
Subject	Due date	Subject	Due date	To-do list
How long?	Start time?	How long?	Start time?	
Materials?		Materials?		
Contact		Contact		
Subject	Due date	Subject	Due date	Saturday schedule
How long?	Start time?	How long?	Start time?	
Materials?		Materials?		
Contact		Contact		
Subject	Due date	Subject	Due date	Sunday schedule
How long?	Start time?	How long?	Start time?	
Materials?		Materials?		
Contact		Contact		
Daily reflection		Daily reflection		Weekend reflection

Key to Questions

How long? *How long will the assignment take?*
Materials? *Do I have all the materials needed to complete the assignment?*

Start time? *When do I plan on starting the assignment?*
Contact? *Who can I contact if I get stuck?*

Daily Planner

<table>
<tr><td>Week of</td><td colspan="2">What am I working on? (Long-term goal)</td></tr>
</table>

Date: **MONDAY**	Date: **TUESDAY**	Date: **WEDNESDAY**
URGENT: REMEMBER THIS!	**URGENT: REMEMBER THIS!**	**URGENT: REMEMBER THIS!**

Subject	Due date	Subject	Due date	Subject	Due date
How long?	Start time?	How long?	Start time?	How long?	Start time?
Materials?		Materials?		Materials?	
Contact		Contact		Contact	

Subject	Due date	Subject	Due date	Subject	Due date
How long?	Start time?	How long?	Start time?	How long?	Start time?
Materials?		Materials?		Materials?	
Contact		Contact		Contact	

Subject	Due date	Subject	Due date	Subject	Due date
How long?	Start time?	How long?	Start time?	How long?	Start time?
Materials?		Materials?		Materials?	
Contact		Contact		Contact	

Subject	Due date	Subject	Due date	Subject	Due date
How long?	Start time?	How long?	Start time?	How long?	Start time?
Materials?		Materials?		Materials?	
Contact		Contact		Contact	

Daily reflection	Daily reflection	Daily reflection

Key to Questions

How long? *How long will the assignment take?*

Materials? *Do I have all the materials needed to complete the assignment?*

Start time? *When do I plan on starting the assignment?*

Contact? *Who can I contact if I get stuck?*

What am I working on? (Long-term goal)

Date: **THURSDAY**		Date: **FRIDAY**		Dates: **SATURDAY & SUNDAY**
URGENT: REMEMBER THIS!		**URGENT: REMEMBER THIS!**		Weekend plans/activities
Subject	Due date	Subject	Due date	
How long?	Start time?	How long?	Start time?	
Materials?		Materials?		
Contact		Contact		
Subject	Due date	Subject	Due date	To-do list
How long?	Start time?	How long?	Start time?	
Materials?		Materials?		
Contact		Contact		
Subject	Due date	Subject	Due date	Saturday schedule
How long?	Start time?	How long?	Start time?	
Materials?		Materials?		
Contact		Contact		
Subject	Due date	Subject	Due date	Sunday schedule
How long?	Start time?	How long?	Start time?	
Materials?		Materials?		
Contact		Contact		
Daily reflection		Daily reflection		Weekend reflection

Key to Questions

How long? *How long will the assignment take?*
Materials? *Do I have all the materials needed to complete the assignment?*

Start time? *When do I plan on starting the assignment?*
Contact? *Who can I contact if I get stuck?*

Daily Planner

Week of	What am I working on? (Long-term goal)

Date: **MONDAY**	Date: **TUESDAY**	Date: **WEDNESDAY**
URGENT: REMEMBER THIS!	URGENT: REMEMBER THIS!	URGENT: REMEMBER THIS!

Subject	Due date	Subject	Due date	Subject	Due date
How long?	Start time?	How long?	Start time?	How long?	Start time?
Materials?		Materials?		Materials?	
Contact		Contact		Contact	

Subject	Due date	Subject	Due date	Subject	Due date
How long?	Start time?	How long?	Start time?	How long?	Start time?
Materials?		Materials?		Materials?	
Contact		Contact		Contact	

Subject	Due date	Subject	Due date	Subject	Due date
How long?	Start time?	How long?	Start time?	How long?	Start time?
Materials?		Materials?		Materials?	
Contact		Contact		Contact	

Subject	Due date	Subject	Due date	Subject	Due date
How long?	Start time?	How long?	Start time?	How long?	Start time?
Materials?		Materials?		Materials?	
Contact		Contact		Contact	

Daily reflection	Daily reflection	Daily reflection

Key to Questions

How long? *How long will the assignment take?*
Materials? *Do I have all the materials needed to complete the assignment?*

Start time? *When do I plan on starting the assignment?*
Contact? *Who can I contact if I get stuck?*

What am I working on? (Long-term goal)

Date: **THURSDAY**		Date: **FRIDAY**		Dates: **SATURDAY & SUNDAY**
URGENT: REMEMBER THIS!		**URGENT: REMEMBER THIS!**		Weekend plans/activities
Subject	Due date	Subject	Due date	
How long?	Start time?	How long?	Start time?	
Materials?		Materials?		
Contact		Contact		
Subject	Due date	Subject	Due date	To-do list
How long?	Start time?	How long?	Start time?	
Materials?		Materials?		
Contact		Contact		
Subject	Due date	Subject	Due date	Saturday schedule
How long?	Start time?	How long?	Start time?	
Materials?		Materials?		
Contact		Contact		
Subject	Due date	Subject	Due date	Sunday schedule
How long?	Start time?	How long?	Start time?	
Materlals?		Materials?		
Contact		Contact		
Daily reflection		Daily reflection		Weekend reflection

Key to Questions

How long? *How long will the assignment take?*   **Start time?** *When do I plan on starting*
Materials? *Do I have all the materials needed*   *the assignment?*
to complete the assignment?   **Contact?** *Who can I contact if I get stuck?*

Daily Planner

Week of	What am I working on? (Long-term goal)

Date: **MONDAY**	Date: **TUESDAY**	Date: **WEDNESDAY**
URGENT: REMEMBER THIS!	**URGENT: REMEMBER THIS!**	**URGENT: REMEMBER THIS!**
Subject / Due date	Subject / Due date	Subject / Due date
How long? / Start time?	How long? / Start time?	How long? / Start time?
Materials?	Materials?	Materials?
Contact	Contact	Contact
Subject / Due date	Subject / Due date	Subject / Due date
How long? / Start time?	How long? / Start time?	How long? / Start time?
Materials?	Materials?	Materials?
Contact	Contact	Contact
Subject / Due date	Subject / Due date	Subject / Due date
How long? / Start time?	How long? / Start time?	How long? / Start time?
Materials?	Materials?	Materials?
Contact	Contact	Contact
Subject / Due date	Subject / Due date	Subject / Due date
How long? / Start time?	How long? / Start time?	How long? / Start time?
Materials?	Materials?	Materials?
Contact	Contact	Contact
Daily reflection	Daily reflection	Daily reflection

Key to Questions

How long? *How long will the assignment take?*
Materials? *Do I have all the materials needed to complete the assignment?*
Start time? *When do I plan on starting the assignment?*
Contact? *Who can I contact if I get stuck?*

What am I working on? (Long-term goal)

Date: **THURSDAY**		Date: **FRIDAY**		Dates: **SATURDAY** & **SUNDAY**
URGENT: REMEMBER THIS!		**URGENT: REMEMBER THIS!**		Weekend plans/activities
Subject	Due date	Subject	Due date	
How long?	Start time?	How long?	Start time?	
Materials?		Materials?		
Contact		Contact		
Subject	Due date	Subject	Due date	To-do list
How long?	Start time?	How long?	Start time?	
Materials?		Materials?		
Contact		Contact		
Subject	Due date	Subject	Due date	Saturday schedule
How long?	Start time?	How long?	Start time?	
Materials?		Materials?		
Contact		Contact		
Subject	Due date	Subject	Due date	Sunday schedule
How long?	Start time?	How long?	Start time?	
Materials?		Materials?		
Contact		Contact		
Daily reflection		Daily reflection		Weekend reflection

Key to Questions

How long? *How long will the assignment take?*
Materials? *Do I have all the materials needed to complete the assignment?*

Start time? *When do I plan on starting the assignment?*
Contact? *Who can I contact if I get stuck?*

Things to Remember for Next Month

(e.g., upcoming projects; midterms, finals or major exams; start of sport season or other extracurricular activity; change in work schedule; family or class trips; school vacation)

Monthly Planner

May 2016

S	M	T	W	T	F	S
1	2	3	4	5	6	7
8	9	10	11	12	13	14
15	16	17	18	19	20	21
22	23	24	25	26	27	28
29	30	31				

May 2017

S	M	T	W	T	F	S
	1	2	3	4	5	6
7	8	9	10	11	12	13
14	15	16	17	18	19	20
21	22	23	24	25	26	27
28	29	30	31			

May 2018

S	M	T	W	T	F	S
		1	2	3	4	5
6	7	8	9	10	11	12
13	14	15	16	17	18	19
20	21	22	23	24	25	26
27	28	29	30	31		

My EXECUTIVE SKILL goal:

My ACADEMIC goal:

**Be sure to check off when you've finished each assignment.
When you hand it in, cross it out!**

Sunday	Monday	Tuesday	Wednesday	Thursday	Friday	Saturday

Daily Planner

Week of
_____

What am I working on? (Long-term goal)
_____

Date: **MONDAY**	Date: **TUESDAY**	Date: **WEDNESDAY**
URGENT: REMEMBER THIS!	**URGENT: REMEMBER THIS!**	**URGENT: REMEMBER THIS!**

Subject	Due date	Subject	Due date	Subject	Due date
How long?	Start time?	How long?	Start time?	How long?	Start time?
Materials?		Materials?		Materials?	
Contact		Contact		Contact	
Subject	Due date	Subject	Due date	Subject	Due date
How long?	Start time?	How long?	Start time?	How long?	Start time?
Materials?		Materials?		Materials?	
Contact		Contact		Contact	
Subject	Due date	Subject	Due date	Subject	Due date
How long?	Start time?	How long?	Start time?	How long?	Start time?
Materials?		Materials?		Materials?	
Contact		Contact		Contact	
Subject	Due date	Subject	Due date	Subject	Due date
How long?	Start time?	How long?	Start time?	How long?	Start time?
Materials?		Materials?		Materials?	
Contact		Contact		Contact	
Daily reflection		Daily reflection		Daily reflection	

Key to Questions

How long? _How long will the assignment take?_

Materials? _Do I have all the materials needed to complete the assignment?_

Start time? _When do I plan on starting the assignment?_

Contact? _Who can I contact if I get stuck?_

What am I working on? (Long-term goal) _____

Date: **THURSDAY**		Date: **FRIDAY**		Dates: **SATURDAY** & **SUNDAY**
URGENT: REMEMBER THIS!		**URGENT: REMEMBER THIS!**		Weekend plans/activities
Subject	Due date	Subject	Due date	
How long?	Start time?	How long?	Start time?	
Materials?		Materials?		
Contact		Contact		
Subject	Due date	Subject	Due date	To-do list
How long?	Start time?	How long?	Start time?	
Materials?		Materials?		
Contact		Contact		
Subject	Due date	Subject	Due date	Saturday schedule
How long?	Start time?	How long?	Start time?	
Materials?		Materials?		
Contact		Contact		
Subject	Due date	Subject	Due date	Sunday schedule
How long?	Start time?	How long?	Start time?	
Materials?		Materials?		
Contact		Contact		
Daily reflection		Daily reflection		Weekend reflection

Key to Questions

How long? _How long will the assignment take?_
Materials? _Do I have all the materials needed to complete the assignment?_

Start time? _When do I plan on starting the assignment?_
Contact? _Who can I contact if I get stuck?_

Daily Planner

Week of
_____

What am I working on? (Long-term goal)
_____

Date: **MONDAY**	Date: **TUESDAY**	Date: **WEDNESDAY**
URGENT: REMEMBER THIS!	**URGENT: REMEMBER THIS!**	**URGENT: REMEMBER THIS!**

Subject	Due date	Subject	Due date	Subject	Due date
How long?	Start time?	How long?	Start time?	How long?	Start time?
Materials?		Materials?		Materials?	
Contact		Contact		Contact	

Subject	Due date	Subject	Due date	Subject	Due date
How long?	Start time?	How long?	Start time?	How long?	Start time?
Materials?		Materials?		Materials?	
Contact		Contact		Contact	

Subject	Due date	Subject	Due date	Subject	Due date
How long?	Start time?	How long?	Start time?	How long?	Start time?
Materials?		Materials?		Materials?	
Contact		Contact		Contact	

Subject	Due date	Subject	Due date	Subject	Due date
How long?	Start time?	How long?	Start time?	How long?	Start time?
Materials?		Materials?		Materials?	
Contact		Contact		Contact	

Daily reflection	Daily reflection	Daily reflection

Key to Questions

How long? _How long will the assignment take?_ **Start time?** _When do I plan on starting_
Materials? _Do I have all the materials needed_   _the assignment?_
to complete the assignment?   **Contact?** _Who can I contact if I get stuck?_

What am I working on? (Long-term goal)

Date: **THURSDAY**		Date: **FRIDAY**		Dates: **SATURDAY** & **SUNDAY**
URGENT: REMEMBER THIS!		**URGENT: REMEMBER THIS!**		Weekend plans/activities
Subject	Due date	Subject	Due date	
How long?	Start time?	How long?	Start time?	
Materials?		Materials?		
Contact		Contact		
Subject	Due date	Subject	Due date	To-do list
How long?	Start time?	How long?	Start time?	
Materials?		Materials?		
Contact		Contact		
Subject	Due date	Subject	Due date	Saturday schedule
How long?	Start time?	How long?	Start time?	
Materials?		Materials?		
Contact		Contact		
Subject	Due date	Subject	Due date	Sunday schedule
How long?	Start time?	How long?	Start time?	
Materials?		Materials?		
Contact		Contact		
Daily reflection		Daily reflection		Weekend reflection

Key to Questions

How long? *How long will the assignment take?*   **Start time?** *When do I plan on starting the assignment?*

Materials? *Do I have all the materials needed to complete the assignment?*   **Contact?** *Who can I contact if I get stuck?*

Daily Planner

Week of _____

What am I working on? (Long-term goal) _____

Date: **MONDAY**	Date: **TUESDAY**	Date: **WEDNESDAY**
URGENT: REMEMBER THIS!	**URGENT: REMEMBER THIS!**	**URGENT: REMEMBER THIS!**

MONDAY		TUESDAY		WEDNESDAY	
Subject	Due date	Subject	Due date	Subject	Due date
How long?	Start time?	How long?	Start time?	How long?	Start time?
Materials?		Materials?		Materials?	
Contact		Contact		Contact	
Subject	Due date	Subject	Due date	Subject	Due date
How long?	Start time?	How long?	Start time?	How long?	Start time?
Materials?		Materials?		Materials?	
Contact		Contact		Contact	
Subject	Due date	Subject	Due date	Subject	Due date
How long?	Start time?	How long?	Start time?	How long?	Start time?
Materials?		Materials?		Materials?	
Contact		Contact		Contact	
Subject	Due date	Subject	Due date	Subject	Due date
How long?	Start time?	How long?	Start time?	How long?	Start time?
Materials?		Materials?		Materials?	
Contact		Contact		Contact	
Daily reflection		Daily reflection		Daily reflection	

Key to Questions

How long? _How long will the assignment take?_   **Start time?** _When do I plan on starting_
Materials? _Do I have all the materials needed_   _the assignment?_
to complete the assignment?   **Contact?** _Who can I contact if I get stuck?_

What am I working on? (Long-term goal)

_____

Date: **THURSDAY**	Date: **FRIDAY**	Dates: **SATURDAY & SUNDAY**
URGENT: REMEMBER THIS!	**URGENT: REMEMBER THIS!**	Weekend plans/activities
Subject / Due date	Subject / Due date	
How long? / Start time?	How long? / Start time?	
Materials?	Materials?	
Contact	Contact	
Subject / Due date	Subject / Due date	To-do list
How long? / Start time?	How long? / Start time?	
Materials?	Materials?	
Contact	Contact	
Subject / Due date	Subject / Due date	Saturday schedule
How long? / Start time?	How long? / Start time?	
Materials?	Materials?	
Contact	Contact	
Subject / Due date	Subject / Due date	Sunday schedule
How long? / Start time?	How long? / Start time?	
Materials?	Materials?	
Contact	Contact	
Daily reflection	Daily reflection	Weekend reflection

Key to Questions

How long? *How long will the assignment take?*
Materials? *Do I have all the materials needed to complete the assignment?*

Start time? *When do I plan on starting the assignment?*
Contact? *Who can I contact if I get stuck?*

Daily Planner

Week of
_____

What am I working on? (Long-term goal)
_____

Date: **MONDAY**	Date: **TUESDAY**	Date: **WEDNESDAY**
URGENT: REMEMBER THIS!	**URGENT: REMEMBER THIS!**	**URGENT: REMEMBER THIS!**

Subject	Due date	Subject	Due date	Subject	Due date

How long?	Start time?	How long?	Start time?	How long?	Start time?
Materials?		Materials?		Materials?	
Contact		Contact		Contact	

Subject	Due date	Subject	Due date	Subject	Due date

How long?	Start time?	How long?	Start time?	How long?	Start time?
Materials?		Materials?		Materials?	
Contact		Contact		Contact	

Subject	Due date	Subject	Due date	Subject	Due date

How long?	Start time?	How long?	Start time?	How long?	Start time?
Materials?		Materials?		Materials?	
Contact		Contact		Contact	

Subject	Due date	Subject	Due date	Subject	Due date

How long?	Start time?	How long?	Start time?	How long?	Start time?
Materials?		Materials?		Materials?	
Contact		Contact		Contact	

Daily reflection	Daily reflection	Daily reflection

Key to Questions

How long? _How long will the assignment take?_   **Start time?** _When do I plan on starting the assignment?_

Materials? _Do I have all the materials needed to complete the assignment?_   **Contact?** _Who can I contact if I get stuck?_

132

What am I working on? (Long-term goal)

Date: **THURSDAY**		Date: **FRIDAY**		Dates: **SATURDAY & SUNDAY**
URGENT: REMEMBER THIS!		**URGENT: REMEMBER THIS!**		Weekend plans/activities
Subject	Due date	Subject	Due date	
How long?	Start time?	How long?	Start time?	
Materials?		Materials?		
Contact		Contact		
Subject	Due date	Subject	Due date	To-do list
How long?	Start time?	How long?	Start time?	
Materials?		Materials?		
Contact		Contact		
Subject	Due date	Subject	Due date	Saturday schedule
How long?	Start time?	How long?	Start time?	
Materials?		Materials?		
Contact		Contact		
Subject	Due date	Subject	Due date	Sunday schedule
How long?	Start time?	How long?	Start time?	
Materials?		Materials?		
Contact		Contact		
Daily reflection		Daily reflection		Weekend reflection

Key to Questions

How long? *How long will the assignment take?*
Materials? *Do I have all the materials needed to complete the assignment?*

Start time? *When do I plan on starting the assignment?*
Contact? *Who can I contact if I get stuck?*

133

Daily Planner

Week of	What am I working on? (Long-term goal)

Date: **MONDAY**	Date: **TUESDAY**	Date: **WEDNESDAY**
URGENT: REMEMBER THIS!	**URGENT: REMEMBER THIS!**	**URGENT: REMEMBER THIS!**

Subject	Due date	Subject	Due date	Subject	Due date
How long?	Start time?	How long?	Start time?	How long?	Start time?
Materials?		Materials?		Materials?	
Contact		Contact		Contact	

Subject	Due date	Subject	Due date	Subject	Due date
How long?	Start time?	How long?	Start time?	How long?	Start time?
Materials?		Materials?		Materials?	
Contact		Contact		Contact	

Subject	Due date	Subject	Due date	Subject	Due date
How long?	Start time?	How long?	Start time?	How long?	Start time?
Materials?		Materials?		Materials?	
Contact		Contact		Contact	

Subject	Due date	Subject	Due date	Subject	Due date
How long?	Start time?	How long?	Start time?	How long?	Start time?
Materials?		Materials?		Materials?	
Contact		Contact		Contact	

Daily reflection	Daily reflection	Daily reflection

Key to Questions

How long? *How long will the assignment take?*   **Start time?** *When do I plan on starting the assignment?*

Materials? *Do I have all the materials needed to complete the assignment?*   **Contact?** *Who can I contact if I get stuck?*

What am I working on? (Long-term goal)

_____

Date: **THURSDAY**		Date: **FRIDAY**		Dates: **SATURDAY & SUNDAY**
URGENT: REMEMBER THIS!		**URGENT: REMEMBER THIS!**		Weekend plans/activities
Subject	Due date	Subject	Due date	
How long?	Start time?	How long?	Start time?	
Materials?		Materials?		
Contact		Contact		
Subject	Due date	Subject	Due date	To-do list
How long?	Start time?	How long?	Start time?	
Materials?		Materials?		
Contact		Contact		
Subject	Due date	Subject	Due date	Saturday schedule
How long?	Start time?	How long?	Start time?	
Materials?		Materials?		
Contact		Contact		
Subject	Due date	Subject	Due date	Sunday schedule
How long?	Start time?	How long?	Start time?	
Materials?		Materials?		
Contact		Contact		
Daily reflection		Daily reflection		Weekend reflection

Key to Questions

How long? _How long will the assignment take?_

Materials? _Do I have all the materials needed to complete the assignment?_

Start time? _When do I plan on starting the assignment?_

Contact? _Who can I contact if I get stuck?_

(e.g., upcoming projects; midterms, finals or major exams; start of sport season or other extracurricular activity; change in work schedule; family or class trips; school vacation)

Monthly Planner

June 2016

S	M	T	W	T	F	S
			1	2	3	4
5	6	7	8	9	10	11
12	13	14	15	16	17	18
19	20	21	22	23	24	25
26	27	28	29	30		

June 2017

S	M	T	W	T	F	S
				1	2	3
4	5	6	7	8	9	10
11	12	13	14	15	16	17
18	19	20	21	22	23	24
25	26	27	28	29	30	

June 2018

S	M	T	W	T	F	S
					1	2
3	4	5	6	7	8	9
10	11	12	13	14	15	16
17	18	19	20	21	22	23
24	25	26	27	28	29	30

My EXECUTIVE SKILL goal:

My ACADEMIC goal:

**Be sure to check off when you've finished each assignment.
When you hand it in, cross it out!**

Sunday	Monday	Tuesday	Wednesday	Thursday	Friday	Saturday

Daily Planner

Week of
_____

What am I working on? (Long-term goal)
_____

Date: **MONDAY**	Date: **TUESDAY**	Date: **WEDNESDAY**
URGENT: REMEMBER THIS!	**URGENT: REMEMBER THIS!**	**URGENT: REMEMBER THIS!**

Subject	Due date	Subject	Due date	Subject	Due date
How long?	Start time?	How long?	Start time?	How long?	Start time?
Materials?		Materials?		Materials?	
Contact		Contact		Contact	

Subject	Due date	Subject	Due date	Subject	Due date
How long?	Start time?	How long?	Start time?	How long?	Start time?
Materials?		Materials?		Materials?	
Contact		Contact		Contact	

Subject	Due date	Subject	Due date	Subject	Due date
How long?	Start time?	How long?	Start time?	How long?	Start time?
Materials?		Materials?		Materials?	
Contact		Contact		Contact	

Subject	Due date	Subject	Due date	Subject	Due date
How long?	Start time?	How long?	Start time?	How long?	Start time?
Materials?		Materials?		Materials?	
Contact		Contact		Contact	

Daily reflection	Daily reflection	Daily reflection

Key to Questions

How long? *How long will the assignment take?*
Materials? *Do I have all the materials needed to complete the assignment?*

Start time? *When do I plan on starting the assignment?*
Contact? *Who can I contact if I get stuck?*

What am I working on? (Long-term goal)

Date: **THURSDAY**	Date: **FRIDAY**	Dates: **SATURDAY & SUNDAY**
URGENT: REMEMBER THIS!	**URGENT: REMEMBER THIS!**	Weekend plans/activities
Subject / Due date	Subject / Duo date	
How long? / Start time?	How long? / Start time?	
Materials?	Materials?	
Contact	Contact	
Subject / Due date	Subject / Due date	To-do list
How long? / Start time?	How long? / Start time?	
Materials?	Materials?	
Contact	Contact	
Subject / Due date	Subject / Due date	Saturday schedule
How long? / Start time?	How long? / Start time?	
Materials?	Materials?	
Contact	Contact	
Subject / Due date	Subject / Due date	Sunday schedule
How long? / Start time?	How long? / Start time?	
Materials?	Materials?	
Contact	Contact	
Daily reflection	Daily reflection	Weekend reflection

Key to Questions

How long? *How long will the assignment take?*
Materials? *Do I have all the materials needed to complete the assignment?*

Start time? *When do I plan on starting the assignment?*
Contact? *Who can I contact if I get stuck?*

Daily Planner

Week of
_____

What am I working on? (Long-term goal)
_____

Date: **MONDAY**	Date: **TUESDAY**	Date: **WEDNESDAY**
URGENT: REMEMBER THIS!	URGENT: REMEMBER THIS!	URGENT: REMEMBER THIS!

MONDAY

Subject	Due date
How long?	Start time?
Materials?	
Contact	

Subject	Due date
How long?	Start time?
Materials?	
Contact	

Subject	Due date
How long?	Start time?
Materials?	
Contact	

Subject	Due date
How long?	Start time?
Materials?	
Contact	

Daily reflection

TUESDAY

Subject	Due date
How long?	Start time?
Materials?	
Contact	

Subject	Due date
How long?	Start time?
Materials?	
Contact	

Subject	Due date
How long?	Start time?
Materials?	
Contact	

Subject	Due date
How long?	Start time?
Materials?	
Contact	

Daily reflection

WEDNESDAY

Subject	Due date
How long?	Start time?
Materials?	
Contact	

Subject	Due date
How long?	Start time?
Materials?	
Contact	

Subject	Due date
How long?	Start time?
Materials?	
Contact	

Subject	Due date
How long?	Start time?
Materials?	
Contact	

Daily reflection

Key to Questions

How long? _How long will the assignment take?_
Materials? _Do I have all the materials needed to complete the assignment?_

Start time? _When do I plan on starting the assignment?_
Contact? _Who can I contact if I get stuck?_

What am I working on? (Long-term goal)

Date: **THURSDAY**	Date: **FRIDAY**	Dates: **SATURDAY & SUNDAY**
URGENT: REMEMBER THIS!	**URGENT: REMEMBER THIS!**	Weekend plans/activities
Subject / Due date	Subject / Due date	
How long? / Start time? Materials? Contact	How long? / Start time? Materials? Contact	
Subject / Due date	Subject / Due date	To-do list
How long? / Start time? Materials? Contact	How long? / Start time? Materials? Contact	
Subject / Due date	Subject / Due date	Saturday schedule
How long? / Start time? Materials? Contact	How long? / Start time? Materials? Contact	
Subject / Due date	Subject / Due date	Sunday schedule
How long? / Start time? Materials? Contact	How long? / Start time? Materials? Contact	
Daily reflection	Daily reflection	Weekend reflection

Key to Questions

How long? *How long will the assignment take?*
Materials? *Do I have all the materials needed to complete the assignment?*

Start time? *When do I plan on starting the assignment?*
Contact? *Who can I contact if I get stuck?*

141

Daily Planner

Week of

What am I working on? (Long-term goal)

Date: **MONDAY**
URGENT: REMEMBER THIS!

Subject	Due date

How long?	Start time?
Materials?	
Contact	

Subject	Due date

How long?	Start time?
Materials?	
Contact	

Subject	Due date

How long?	Start time?
Materials?	
Contact	

Subject	Due date

How long?	Start time?
Materials?	
Contact	

Daily reflection

Date: **TUESDAY**
URGENT: REMEMBER THIS!

Subject	Due date

How long?	Start time?
Materials?	
Contact	

Subject	Due date

How long?	Start time?
Materials?	
Contact	

Subject	Due date

How long?	Start time?
Materials?	
Contact	

Subject	Due date

How long?	Start time?
Materials?	
Contact	

Daily reflection

Date: **WEDNESDAY**
URGENT: REMEMBER THIS!

Subject	Due date

How long?	Start time?
Materials?	
Contact	

Subject	Due date

How long?	Start time?
Materials?	
Contact	

Subject	Due date

How long?	Start time?
Materials?	
Contact	

Subject	Due date

How long?	Start time?
Materials?	
Contact	

Daily reflection

Key to Questions

How long? *How long will the assignment take?*
Materials? *Do I have all the materials needed to complete the assignment?*

Start time? *When do I plan on starting the assignment?*
Contact? *Who can I contact if I get stuck?*

What am I working on? (Long-term goal)

Date: **THURSDAY**		Date: **FRIDAY**		Dates: **SATURDAY** & **SUNDAY**
URGENT: REMEMBER THIS!		**URGENT: REMEMBER THIS!**		Weekend plans/activities
Subject	Due date	Subject	Due date	
How long?	Start time?	How long?	Start time?	
Materials?		Materials?		
Contact		Contact		
Subject	Due date	Subject	Due date	To-do list
How long?	Start time?	How long?	Start time?	
Materials?		Materials?		
Contact		Contact		
Subject	Due date	Subject	Due date	Saturday schedule
How long?	Start time?	How long?	Start time?	
Materials?		Materials?		
Contact		Contact		
Subject	Due date	Subject	Due date	Sunday schedule
How long?	Start time?	How long?	Start time?	
Materials?		Materials?		
Contact		Contact		
Daily reflection		Daily reflection		Weekend reflection

Key to Questions

How long? *How long will the assignment take?*
Materials? *Do I have all the materials needed to complete the assignment?*

Start time? *When do I plan on starting the assignment?*
Contact? *Who can I contact if I get stuck?*

143

Daily Planner

Week of	What am I working on? (Long-term goal)

Date: **MONDAY**	Date: **TUESDAY**	Date: **WEDNESDAY**
URGENT: REMEMBER THIS!	**URGENT: REMEMBER THIS!**	**URGENT: REMEMBER THIS!**

Subject	Due date	Subject	Due date	Subject	Due date

How long?	Start time?	How long?	Start time?	How long?	Start time?
Materials?		Materials?		Materials?	
Contact		Contact		Contact	

Subject	Due date	Subject	Due date	Subject	Due date

How long?	Start time?	How long?	Start time?	How long?	Start time?
Materials?		Materials?		Materials?	
Contact		Contact		Contact	

Subject	Due date	Subject	Due date	Subject	Due date

How long?	Start time?	How long?	Start time?	How long?	Start time?
Materials?		Materials?		Materials?	
Contact		Contact		Contact	

Subject	Due date	Subject	Due date	Subject	Due date

How long?	Start time?	How long?	Start time?	How long?	Start time?
Materials?		Materials?		Materials?	
Contact		Contact		Contact	
Daily reflection		Daily reflection		Daily reflection	

Key to Questions

How long? *How long will the assignment take?*
Materials? *Do I have all the materials needed to complete the assignment?*

Start time? *When do I plan on starting the assignment?*
Contact? *Who can I contact if I get stuck?*

What am I working on? (Long-term goal)

Date: **THURSDAY**	Date: **FRIDAY**	Dates: **SATURDAY** & **SUNDAY**
URGENT: REMEMBER THIS!	**URGENT: REMEMBER THIS!**	Weekend plans/activities
Subject / Due date	Subject / Due date	
How long? / Start time?	How long? / Start time?	
Materials?	Materials?	
Contact	Contact	
Subject / Due date	Subject / Due date	To-do list
How long? / Start time?	How long? / Start time?	
Materials?	Materials?	
Contact	Contact	
Subject / Due date	Subject / Due date	Saturday schedule
How long? / Start time?	How long? / Start time?	
Materials?	Materials?	
Contact	Contact	
Subject / Due date	Subject / Due date	Sunday schedule
How long? / Start time?	How long? / Start time?	
Materials?	Materials?	
Contact	Contact	
Daily reflection	Daily reflection	Weekend reflection

Key to Questions

How long? *How long will the assignment take?*   **Start time?** *When do I plan on starting the assignment?*
Materials? *Do I have all the materials needed to complete the assignment?*   **Contact?** *Who can I contact if I get stuck?*

145

Monthly Planner

July 2016

S	M	T	W	T	F	S
					1	2
3	4	5	6	7	8	9
10	11	12	13	14	15	16
17	18	19	20	21	22	23
24	25	26	27	28	29	30
31						

July 2017

S	M	T	W	T	F	S
						1
2	3	4	5	6	7	8
9	10	11	12	13	14	15
16	17	18	19	20	21	22
23	24	25	26	27	28	29
30	31					

July 2018

S	M	T	W	T	F	S
1	2	3	4	5	6	7
8	9	10	11	12	13	14
15	16	17	18	19	20	21
22	23	24	25	26	27	28
29	30	31				

My EXECUTIVE SKILL goal:

My ACADEMIC goal:

**Be sure to check off when you've finished each assignment.
When you hand it in, <u>cross it out</u>!**

Sunday	Monday	Tuesday	Wednesday	Thursday	Friday	Saturday

PART IV

Strategies for Success

This part includes templates and brief descriptions of a variety of strategies to help with things such as writing papers, planning long-term projects, studying for tests, reading for comprehension, note taking, proofreading, and staying organized.

The first three forms (Studying for Tests, Five-Paragraph Essay Template, and Long-Term-Project Planning Form) give you several copies of templates you can use. Having them in the planner gives you a permanent record and makes them harder to lose (unless you lose the planner). As the year goes along, you may run out of these, so feel free to photocopy them and keep copies in your binder. Or you can download copies at *www.guilford.com/dawson6-forms*.

The section on Other Strategies includes brief descriptions of strategies you might use for other kinds of assignments. You may realize that you don't know how to do things that teachers expect you to do (such as read for comprehension, take notes, write a summary). This section gives you some ideas for how to do these things. If you're not happy with any of the suggestions, you may want to do an Internet search of the topic to find other study strategies that would work better for you.

Contents

Studying for Tests

Test date: _____ Subject: _____

Check off the strategies you will use.	
____ 1. Reread text	____ 13. Study flash cards
____ 2. Reread/organize notes	____ 14. Memorize/rehearse
____ 3. Read/recite main points	____ 15. Create a "cheat sheet"
____ 4. Outline text	____ 16. Study with friend
____ 5. Highlight text	____ 17. Study with study group
____ 6. Highlight notes	____ 18. Study session with teacher
____ 7. Use study guide	____ 19. Study with a parent
____ 8. Make concept maps	____ 20. Ask for help
____ 9. Make lists/organize	____ 21. Use Quizlet
____ 10. Take practice test	____ 22. Do practice problems when studying for STEM (science, technology, engineering, and math) subjects
____ 11. Quiz myself	
____ 12. Have someone else quiz me	____ 23. Other: _____

Study Plan

Date	Day	Which strategies will I use? (Write number)	How much time for each strategy?
	4 days before test	1. 2. 3.	1. 2. 3.
	3 days before test	1. 2. 3.	1. 2. 3.

Studying for Tests *(cont.)*

Date	Day	Which strategies will I use? (Write number)	How much time for each strategy?
	2 days before test	1. 2. 3.	1. 2. 3.
	1 day before test	1. 2. 3.	1. 2. 3.

Posttest Evaluation

How did your studying work out? Answer the following questions:

1. What strategies worked best?

2. What strategies were not so helpful?

3. Did you spend enough time studying? Yes No

4. If no, what more should you have done?

5. What will you do differently the next time?

Studying for Tests

Test date: _____   Subject: _____

Check off the strategies you will use.	
____ 1. Reread text	____ 13. Study flash cards
____ 2. Reread/organize notes	____ 14. Memorize/rehearse
____ 3. Read/recite main points	____ 15. Create a "cheat sheet"
____ 4. Outline text	____ 16. Study with friend
____ 5. Highlight text	____ 17. Study with study group
____ 6. Highlight notes	____ 18. Study session with teacher
____ 7. Use study guide	____ 19. Study with a parent
____ 8. Make concept maps	____ 20. Ask for help
____ 9. Make lists/organize	____ 21. Use Quizlet
____ 10. Take practice test	____ 22. Do practice problems when studying for STEM (science, technology, engineering, and math) subjects
____ 11. Quiz myself	
____ 12. Have someone else quiz me	____ 23. Other: _____

Study Plan

Date	Day	Which strategies will I use? (Write number)	How much time for each strategy?
	4 days before test	1. 2. 3.	1. 2. 3.
	3 days before test	1. 2. 3.	1. 2. 3.

Studying for Tests (cont.)

Date	Day	Which strategies will I use? (Write number)	How much time for each strategy?
	2 days before test	1. 2. 3.	1. 2. 3.
	1 day before test	1. 2. 3.	1. 2. 3.

Posttest Evaluation

How did your studying work out? Answer the following questions:

1. What strategies worked best?

2. What strategies were not so helpful?

3. Did you spend enough time studying? Yes No

4. If no, what more should you have done?

5. What will you do differently the next time?

Studying for Tests

Test date: _____   **Subject:** _____

Check off the strategies you will use.

____ 1. Reread text	____ 13. Study flash cards
____ 2. Reread/organize notes	____ 14. Memorize/rehearse
____ 3. Read/recite main points	____ 15. Create a "cheat sheet"
____ 4. Outline text	____ 16. Study with friend
____ 5. Highlight text	____ 17. Study with study group
____ 6. Highlight notes	____ 18. Study session with teacher
____ 7. Use study guide	____ 19. Study with a parent
____ 8. Make concept maps	____ 20. Ask for help
____ 9. Make lists/organize	____ 21. Use Quizlet
____ 10. Take practice test	____ 22. Do practice problems when studying for STEM (science, technology, engineering, and math) subjects
____ 11. Quiz myself	
____ 12. Have someone else quiz me	____ 23. Other: _____

Study Plan

Date	Day	Which strategies will I use? (Write number)	How much time for each strategy?
	4 days before test	1. 2. 3.	1. 2. 3.
	3 days before test	1. 2. 3.	1. 2. 3.

Studying for Tests (cont.)

Date	Day	Which strategies will I use? (Write number)	How much time for each strategy?
	2 days before test	1. 2. 3.	1. 2. 3.
	1 day before test	1. 2. 3.	1. 2. 3.

Posttest Evaluation

How did your studying work out? Answer the following questions:

1. What strategies worked best?

2. What strategies were not so helpful?

3. Did you spend enough time studying? Yes No

4. If no, what more should you have done?

5. What will you do differently the next time?

Studying for Tests

Test date: _____   Subject: _____

Check off the strategies you will use.	
_____ 1. Reread text	_____ 13. Study flash cards
_____ 2. Reread/organize notes	_____ 14. Memorize/rehearse
_____ 3. Read/recite main points	_____ 15. Create a "cheat sheet"
_____ 4. Outline text	_____ 16. Study with friend
_____ 5. Highlight text	_____ 17. Study with study group
_____ 6. Highlight notes	_____ 18. Study session with teacher
_____ 7. Use study guide	_____ 19. Study with a parent
_____ 8. Make concept maps	_____ 20. Ask for help
_____ 9. Make lists/organize	_____ 21. Use Quizlet
_____ 10. Take practice test	_____ 22. Do practice problems when studying for STEM (science, technology, engineering, and math) subjects
_____ 11. Quiz myself	
_____ 12. Have someone else quiz me	_____ 23. Other: _____

Study Plan

Date	Day	Which strategies will I use? (Write number)	How much time for each strategy?
	4 days before test	1. 2. 3.	1. 2. 3.
	3 days before test	1. 2. 3.	1. 2. 3.

Studying for Tests (cont.)

Date	Day	Which strategies will I use? (Write number)	How much time for each strategy?
	2 days before test	1. 2. 3.	1. 2. 3.
	1 day before test	1. 2. 3.	1. 2. 3.

Posttest Evaluation

How did your studying work out? Answer the following questions:

1. What strategies worked best?

2. What strategies were not so helpful?

3. Did you spend enough time studying? Yes No

4. If no, what more should you have done?

5. What will you do differently the next time?

Studying for Tests

Test date: _____   Subject: _____

Check off the strategies you will use.	
_____ 1. Reread text	_____ 13. Study flash cards
_____ 2. Reread/organize notes	_____ 14. Memorize/rehearse
_____ 3. Read/recite main points	_____ 15. Create a "cheat sheet"
_____ 4. Outline text	_____ 16. Study with friend
_____ 5. Highlight text	_____ 17. Study with study group
_____ 6. Highlight notes	_____ 18. Study session with teacher
_____ 7. Use study guide	_____ 19. Study with a parent
_____ 8. Make concept maps	_____ 20. Ask for help
_____ 9. Make lists/organize	_____ 21. Use Quizlet
_____ 10. Take practice test	_____ 22. Do practice problems when studying for STEM (science, technology, engineering, and math) subjects
_____ 11. Quiz myself	
_____ 12. Have someone else quiz me	_____ 23. Other: _____

Study Plan

Date	Day	Which strategies will I use? (Write number)	How much time for each strategy?
	4 days before test	1. 2. 3.	1. 2. 3.
	3 days before test	1. 2. 3.	1. 2. 3.

Studying for Tests (cont.)

Date	Day	Which strategies will I use? (Write number)	How much time for each strategy?
	2 days before test	1. 2. 3.	1. 2. 3.
	1 day before test	1. 2. 3.	1. 2. 3.

Posttest Evaluation

How did your studying work out? Answer the following questions:

1. What strategies worked best?

2. What strategies were not so helpful?

3. Did you spend enough time studying? Yes No

4. If no, what more should you have done?

5. What will you do differently the next time?

Five-Paragraph Essay Template

Due Date: _____

Introductory Paragraph

Sentence 1 summarizes what your essay is about:

Sentence 2 focuses in on the main point you want to make:

Sentence 3 adds more detail or explains why the topic is important:

Body Paragraphs

Paragraph 1, topic sentence:

Supporting detail 1:

Supporting detail 2:

Supporting detail 3:

Five-Paragraph Essay Template (cont.)

Paragraph 2, topic sentence:

    Supporting detail 1:

    Supporting detail 2:

    Supporting detail 3:

Paragraph 3, topic sentence:

    Supporting detail 1:

    Supporting detail 2:

    Supporting detail 3:

Concluding Paragraph

Restate the most important point you want to make in the paper (what the reader should go away understanding):

Five-Paragraph Essay Template

Due Date: _____

From *The Work-Smart Academic Planner*. Copyright 2015 by The Guilford Press.

Paragraph 2, topic sentence:

Supporting detail 1:

Supporting detail 2:

Supporting detail 3:

Paragraph 3, topic sentence:

Supporting detail 1:

Supporting detail 2:

Supporting detail 3:

Concluding Paragraph

Restate the most important point you want to make in the paper (what the reader should go away understanding):

Five-Paragraph Essay Template

Due Date: _____

Sentence 1 summarizes what your essay is about:

Sentence 2 focuses in on the main point you want to make:

Sentence 3 adds more detail or explains why the topic is important:

Body Paragraphs

Paragraph 1, topic sentence:

    Supporting detail 1:

    Supporting detail 2:

    Supporting detail 3:

Five-Paragraph Essay Template (cont.)

Paragraph 2, topic sentence:

Supporting detail 1:

Supporting detail 2:

Supporting detail 3:

Paragraph 3, topic sentence:

Supporting detail 1:

Supporting detail 2:

Supporting detail 3:

Concluding Paragraph

Restate the most important point you want to make in the paper (what the reader should go away understanding):

Five-Paragraph Essay Template

Due Date: _____

Introductory Paragraph

Sentence 1 summarizes what your essay is about:

Sentence 2 focuses in on the main point you want to make:

Sentence 3 adds more detail or explains why the topic is important:

Body Paragraphs

Paragraph 1, topic sentence:

    Supporting detail 1:

    Supporting detail 2:

    Supporting detail 3:

Paragraph 2, topic sentence:

Supporting detail 1:

Supporting detail 2:

Supporting detail 3:

Paragraph 3, topic sentence:

Supporting detail 1:

Supporting detail 2:

Supporting detail 3:

Concluding Paragraph

Restate the most important point you want to make in the paper (what the reader should go away understanding):

Five-Paragraph Essay Template

Due Date: _____

Introductory Paragraph

Sentence 1 summarizes what your essay is about:

Sentence 2 focuses in on the main point you want to make:

Sentence 3 adds more detail or explains why the topic is important:

Body Paragraphs

Paragraph 1, topic sentence:

    Supporting detail 1:

    Supporting detail 2:

    Supporting detail 3:

Paragraph 2, topic sentence:

    Supporting detail 1:

    Supporting detail 2:

    Supporting detail 3:

Paragraph 3, topic sentence:

    Supporting detail 1:

    Supporting detail 2:

    Supporting detail 3:

Concluding Paragraph

Restate the most important point you want to make in the paper (what the reader should go **away** understanding):

Long-Term-Project Planning Form

Due Date: _____

Step 1: Select a Topic

What are possible topics?	What I like about this choice:	What I don't like:
1.		
2.		
3.		
4.		
5.		

Final topic choice:

Step 2: Identify Necessary Materials

What materials or resources do I need?	Where will I get them?	When will I get them?
1.		
2.		
3.		
4.		
5.		

Long-Term–Project Planning Form (cont.)

What do I need to do? (List each step in order)	When will I do it?	Check off when done
Step 1:		
Step 2:		
Step 3:		
Step 4:		
Step 5:		
Step 6:		
Step 7:		
Step 8:		
Step 9:		
Step 10:		

Reminder List: Include here any additional tasks or details you need to keep in mind as you work on the project. Cross out or check each one off as you take care of it.

____ 1.

____ 2.

____ 3.

____ 4.

____ 5.

____ 6.

____ 7.

____ 8.

____ 9.

____ 10.

Long-Term-Project Planning Form

Due Date: _____

Step 1: Select a Topic

What are possible topics?	What I like about this choice:	What I don't like:
1.		
2.		
3.		
4.		
5.		

Final topic choice:

Step 2: Identify Necessary Materials

What materials or resources do I need?	Where will I get them?	When will I get them?
1.		
2.		
3.		
4.		
5.		

Long-Term-Project Planning Form (cont.)

What do I need to do? (List each step in order)	When will I do it?	Check off when done
Step 1:		
Step 2:		
Step 3:		
Step 4:		
Step 5:		
Step 6:		
Step 7:		
Step 8:		
Step 9:		
Step 10:		

Reminder List: Include here any additional tasks or details you need to keep in mind as you work on the project. Cross out or check each one off as you take care of it.

_____ 1.

_____ 2.

_____ 3.

_____ 4.

_____ 5.

_____ 6.

_____ 7.

_____ 8.

_____ 9.

_____ 10.

Long-Term-Project Planning Form

Due Date: _____

Step 1: Select a Topic

What are possible topics?	What I like about this choice:	What I don't like:
1.		
2.		
3.		
4.		
5.		

Final topic choice:

Step 2: Identify Necessary Materials

What materials or resources do I need?	Where will I get them?	When will I get them?
1.		
2.		
3.		
4.		
5.		

Long-Term-Project Planning Form (cont.)

What do I need to do? (List each step in order)	When will I do it?	Check off when done
Step 1:		
Step 2:		
Step 3:		
Step 4:		
Step 5:		
Step 6:		
Step 7:		
Step 8:		
Step 9:		
Step 10:		

Reminder List: Include here any additional tasks or details you need to keep in mind as you work on the project. Cross out or check each one off as you take care of it.

____ 1.

____ 2.

____ 3.

____ 4.

____ 5.

____ 6.

____ 7.

____ 8.

____ 9.

____ 10.

Long-Term-Project Planning Form

Due Date: _____

Step 1: Select a Topic

What are possible topics?	What I like about this choice:	What I don't like:
1.		
2.		
3.		
4.		
5.		

Final topic choice:

Step 2: Identify Necessary Materials

What materials or resources do I need?	Where will I get them?	When will I get them?
1.		
2.		
3.		
4.		
5.		

Long-Term-Project Planning Form *(cont.)*

Step 3: Identify Project Tasks and Due Dates

What do I need to do? (List each step in order)	When will I do it?	Check off when done
Step 1:		
Step 2:		
Step 3:		
Step 4:		
Step 5:		
Step 6:		
Step 7:		
Step 8:		
Step 9:		
Step 10:		

Reminder List: Include here any additional tasks or details you need to keep in mind as you work on the project. Cross out or check each one off as you take care of it.

_____ 1.

_____ 2.

_____ 3.

_____ 4.

_____ 5.

_____ 6.

_____ 7.

_____ 8.

_____ 9.

_____ 10.

Long-Term-Project Planning Form

Due Date: _____

Long-Term-Project Planning Form (cont.)

What do I need to do? (List each step in order)	When will I do it?	Check off when done
Step 1:		
Step 2:		
Step 3:		
Step 4:		
Step 5:		
Step 6:		
Step 7:		
Step 8:		
Step 9:		
Step 10:		

Reminder List: Include here any additional tasks or details you need to keep in mind as you work on the project. Cross out or check each one off as you take care of it.

_____ 1.

_____ 2.

_____ 3.

_____ 4.

_____ 5.

_____ 6.

_____ 7.

_____ 8.

_____ 9.

_____ 10.

Other Strategies

SMART (Self-Monitoring Approach to Reading and Thinking)

- While you're reading, place a check mark in the margin next to things you understand.

- Place a question mark in the margin next to anything you don't understand.

- When you've finished a section, summarize in your own words what you understand.

- Take another look at what you didn't understand—reread those parts and try to figure out why you don't understand it. See if you can make an association to material or concepts you do understand.

SQ3R (Survey, Question, Read, Recite, Review)

- **Survey:** Look through the entire chapter to get an overall sense of what the material is about. Look at headings, graphs, charts, and pictures for clues.

- **Question:** Turn each heading into a question that you will then read to answer.

- **Read:** Read the material to find the answers to the questions you've generated.

- **Recite:** At the end of each section, see if you can answer the questions in that section without looking back. Look back for the answers to any questions you were unable to answer.

- **Review:** When you're done, go back over the questions and try to answer them one more time.

K–W–L

This approach begins with activating any background knowledge (**K**) you may have related to the topic you are reading about. Jot down notes that highlight what you know (e.g., key words, shorthand references). Then generate a list of what you would like to know about the topic (**W**). This might be a series of questions or topic areas. Then read the material, and finally summarize what you have learned (**L**). Again, these could be key words or shorthand references. Write a summary of (or summarize aloud) the material you have read.

Know	Want to learn	Learned

Three-Color Highlighting

As you read, use a different color highlighter for these three categories of information:

- Main points (often the first or last paragraph in a section or the first sentence in a paragraph)

- Supporting details (elaborates on the main points, provides evidence or proof to support assertions or opinions)

- Terms (key vocabulary or concepts)

How to Write a Summary

1. Identify the topic being summarized.

2. Write the main idea of the passage.

3. Include important details that support the main idea.

4. Arrange them in a logical order.

5. Reread to make sure it makes sense and covers the most important information.

How to Take Good Notes (the Cornell Method)

1. Divide lined paper into three columns.

2. In the center column, write down what the teacher is saying in the sequence given.

3. In the left-hand column, write key concepts and "big ideas."

4. In the right-hand column, jot down a word or two that captures a personal experience related to the topic.

5. The center column is completed during class.

6. The side columns can be completed in class, as well as when you review your notes after class or when studying for a test.

Key terms	Running notes	Reflections/ experiences

Proofreading Checklist

_____ Do all sentences begin with a capital letter?

_____ Did I capitalize all proper nouns?

_____ Are all sentences complete sentences (no run-ons or sentence fragments)?

_____ Did I divide my writing into paragraphs (one key idea per paragraph)?

_____ Do all sentences have ending punctuation (. ? !)?

_____ Did I use commas and quotation marks correctly?

_____ Did I spell every word correctly?

How to Stay Organized and Keep Track of Materials

What works for another student may not work for you, but here's an approach to try:

1. Use one large binder for all subjects, using a tab divider for each subject. The binder should come with pockets in the front and back.

2. Write INCOMPLETE HOMEWORK on the front pocket and put any homework

assignments you get there as soon as the teacher hands them out. Write COMPLETED HOMEWORK on the back pocket.

3. Write the DUE DATE for homework assignments on the top of the sheet as soon as you get it.

4. Organize homework in the INCOMPLETE HOMEWORK pocket by due date, with the one due first on top. As soon as you open your binder for whatever reason, you'll see the assignment and the due date to help you remember to do it.

5. As soon as you finish a homework assignment, put it in the COMPLETED HOMEWORK pocket.

6. Keep all papers your teacher wants you to keep in the section for that class. Throw out papers you don't have to keep. You may want to check with the teacher if you're not sure whether you should save something.

7. You may also want to include in the binder a zippered pouch with materials such as pens, pencils, erasers, and calculators.

How to Manage Distractions

Contrary to popular belief, the brain actually CAN'T multitask. What you're really doing when you think you're multitasking is jumping back and forth very quickly between the tasks you're working on. It turns out this is a very inefficient way for the brain to process information or manage output. For teenagers, the most common distraction while studying is technology (surfing the 'Net; texting; managing social media such as Facebook, Twitter, Instagram, and so forth). Playing video games and watching TV are also common distractions. Here are some ways you might want to consider to manage these distractions:

1. Rather than jumping back and forth between homework and technology, *take technology breaks*. Decide how long you think you can focus before you need a break and set the timer on your smartphone. Work until the timer goes off, then set the timer to limit your technology break.

2. Rather than working for a set amount of time, set a work goal that you plan to accomplish before taking a break. For example, you may decide to finish half of your math assignment before breaking.

3. Do homework with a friend, with both of you agreeing to work for a set amount of time or to complete specific work goals before breaking. Also agree on how long the breaks will last.

4. Use technology to *screen out* distractions rather than create them. Some students, for instance, find they can listen to instrumental music on their iPods but can't listen to music with lyrics because they start thinking about the words when the music includes lyrics.

5. If you get bored working on one task for a long time, think about switching off between different homework assignments to break up the tedium. If you have a lot of homework and not a lot of time, this may work better than taking a complete break from studying.

6. As an alternative to technology breaks, take an exercise break. Research shows that physical exercise can improve attention, so you may want to try taking 10-minute breaks to shoot baskets, play foosball, lift weights, go on the treadmill, or play a Wii game that involves exercise.

How to Manage Your Time

Time management is actually composed of other executive skills—task initiation, sustained attention, and planning—as well as a unique element called time estimation. Many students have trouble with time management because they're not good at estimating how long something will take. Most frequently, they *underestimate* how long a difficult task will take and so don't build in enough time to get it done. Occasionally, students *overestimate* how long the task will take, which leads them to delay starting because they feel overwhelmed by it. Time estimation can be improved through practice, which is why the daily planner includes a space for you to estimate how long you think any given homework assignment will take. If you track your estimate to see whether it was correct or not, you can improve your time estimation skills.

Other strategies for improving time management skills are:

1. Try to stick to a predictable schedule, particularly for studying, but also for sleep and other daily routines. Build reasonable "down time" into your daily routines.

2. Make a public commitment to follow your schedule—for instance, you might tell your mom on Saturday the time you plan to study for a test or begin writing a paper during the weekend. You may even ask her to remind you when the time comes.

3. Set alarms or use a reminder program on your smartphone to get you started on time.

4. Create checklists or to-do lists that include start times and an estimate of how long the task will take. Add up the amount of time needed to get through the list and delete things if the list is not realistic.